Edubooks by Kathy S. Thompson

A Journey through the Triangle of Canada, Britain, and America
Afterlife Envision
Brown Flowers in Gloucester (Drama)
Cataract Surgery Is No Fun
Counseling Helps (27 Helps)
Creeping Greed
Crime and Rehabilitation (and The Gap Theory)
Crimes, Crime Awareness, and Crime Prevention, including the Mafia
Diary of a Drug Addict
8 Drama Stories: Twists and Turns
Funeral Planning, Memorial Services, and Coping with Grief
Global Warming Causes, Solutions, and Theories
I Care For My Cats (and Other Animals)
Landscaping a Small Lot
Letters to England
Living and Travelling in the South-West
Political Write-ups
Racial Equality
13 Science Fiction Stories: Separate Worlds
Scriptwriters and Scriptwriting
Sex Trends in Society
Shingles are Awful
Stair-Temple Sites/Chilean Easter Island
Stonehenge and Other Stone-Placement Sites
Taking a Shower—Shower Savvy
The Case Study—Case by Case
The Equal Personage Concept of Children and Youth (EPCCY)
The Gap Theory for Mental Assessment and Treatment
The Outdoor Perils of Cats
The Surgery Experience
Three Careers and a Driven Life: The Life of My Father
Travellers (Sci Fi)
Writers and Writing

Poems and Short Works Books (57 in each, plus Intros)

Going through Life Poems and Short Works
Getting through Life Poems and Short Works
Next Poems and Short Works
Straggler Poems and Short Works
Isolates Poems and Short Works
Extra Poems and Short Works
Final Poems and Short Works
Spare Poems and Short Works
Subsequent Poems and Short Works (partial)

Young Readers Books

Charlie and Mom Cat (early readers)
The Cygnet (young readers, and all ages)
Madame Spider (tweens, teens, and all ages)
Philpot and the Forest Animals (young readers, and all ages)

SHINGLES ARE AWFUL

THE MANAGEMENT OF A VIRUS

KATHY S. THOMPSON, M.A.,
EDUCATION AND COUNSELING

authorHOUSE

AuthorHouse™
1663 Liberty Drive
Bloomington, IN 47403
www.authorhouse.com
Phone: 833-262-8899

Published by AuthorHouse 11/23/2022

ISBN: 978-1-6655-3805-3 (sc)
ISBN: 978-1-6655-3817-6 (e)

Library of Congress Control Number: 2021918846

Print information available on the last page.

Any people depicted in stock imagery provided by Getty Images are models, and such images are being used for illustrative purposes only. Certain stock imagery © Getty Images.

This book is printed on acid-free paper.

CONTENTS

DISCLAIMER

The author makes no claim to the accuracy of all details in this book. The author has attempted to remove any noted errors and has checked out what could be checked out, as well as possible. Efforts towards accuracy have been made but the author makes no claim to there being full and complete accuracy of all the book's contents. Any errors brought to the attention of the author will be corrected in the future.

Any medical-related content in this book is not intended to supplant any type of medical orientation or treatment from a licensed medical authority. It is intended to support it. I pose a number of rhetorical medical questions, many of which I don't answer or answer in entirety. The information, ideas, and suggestions in this book are not intended as a substitute for professional medical advice. Before following any suggestions explained in the book, you should consult your personal physician. Neither the author nor the publisher shall be liable or responsible for any loss or damage allegedly arising as a consequence of your use or application of any information or suggestions in this book. When there is a medical issue or disorder, always seek advice and help from a licensed physician or health-care provider.

APOLOGY

I know this book is not perfectly written. Though I majored in English as an undergraduate, I've forgotten some grammar, plus some grammar and even spelling rules have changed over the years and I have not kept up with those new ways, although, many of them are optional. Still, grammar can get to be a little muddled in the mind. So, apologies for any and all imperfections. Just getting the book out was the priority. Therefore, you may find some irregularity, in that the book was not professionally edited. I hope there's no typing errors (but my eyes are not so good). So, apologies go out for any and all oversights or undersights. There may be some repetition, too. Some is purposely there, to drive in a point. Some is accidentally there but is put in a different context. Because I was working on more than one book at a time, I would sometimes forget what I had already written so I occasionally put the same information in twice—almost always in a different context. Also, this book was a bit of a rush job. Because the book was somewhat rushed, all sentence construction may not be immaculate but most of the content generally makes sense in so far as I know.

Furthermore, you may think some text information does not directly relate to the included covered subjects. There is, perhaps, some borderline material in there. With what may seem extraneous, if you give it more thought, you would likely make the connection that the material does relate to the overall subject and certainly to what is generally being covered in the text. There are one or two covered areas that may be more remotely related to the principal subject but I wanted to add in those subjects and felt that they were connected. All points made tie in with the overall subject, and they generally or specifically relate. Some points that were made do, more than others. I tried to be thorough; I am a detail-oriented writer. Putting so many details in so the book would be more comprehensive was not always so easy to do and so the organization of the book is not quite all that I would have wanted it to be, but I'm not unhappy with it. Mainly, I got everything in that I wanted in and that was my priority. Again, this book was a little rushed.

Because the author was finishing up so many books at the same time, because of her age and the COVID scare, and because of her optical deterioration (she is legally blind in one eye), there could be a few typing or grammar errors in one or more texts of her books. They'll be a bit like looking for a needle in a haystack but some could be there, even though efforts were made to spot check for them and remove them.

DEDICATION

To all people who have suffered from the ordeal of having shingles; it is more of an ordeal than most people realize.

Also to Bob, Jeanne, Margaret, Nick, Anna, Greg, and Jim—helpful friends along the way.

AUTHOR'S NOTE

The shingles virus just secretly and quietly lives in the body for many years until something suddenly upsets it, usually after a person gets to be around age fifty; it particularly gets agitated when people are in their seventies and even eighties but there are many recorded cases of people who were in their sixties and a little less so, of people who were in their fifties. Some get shingles when they are ninety or over ninety, but fewer people are alive at that age so you would have to look at per-capita statistics (per head count) to know what the percentage index would be for that age group and as to how it would compare with other age groups. It would be somewhat high. All these age groups would not have had access to the chickenpox immunization when they were young. It was not around when some and certain people were in school or were getting their shots and were young. Today, some schools may not administer the immunization, but children need to have it administered while they are young. It should be a required immunization when children are young. It should be free, by way of elementary schools.

PART 1
Early onset of the virus, and initial experiences

All the people I've spoken to recently did not know what shingles were, and I do mean all. They had heard the word, but only two knew they were painful and they really didn't know what they were or why they were painful. No one knew it was a virus. No one knew much of anything about the disease. I decided there was too much of a knowledge gap concerning the subject for me to not do a write-up about them. I wanted to keep the write-up brief and general and non-technical, medically. I wanted to, generally, write the book by way of a layperson's perspective, since I am not a medical professional. I simply wanted to record the experiences I'd had and stick to the basics. Some basic medical is in the book, though, and I include some medical details. As an educator, I know how important the accumulation of knowledge is.

<u>The mainstream needs to be informed about shingles because so few know about shingles.</u> Many people out there got chickenpox and they never had the chickenpox immunization so they are carrying the shingles-related virus and could get these awful shingles, particularly after age 50. Few get shingles before age 50, but this does happen. It all depends on the strength of the immune system and as a person ages, their immune system can lose strength, which we've all seen with the coronavirus (COVID-19 and it variants and sub-variants) because it has tended to take over and more readily cause the death of the elderly.

The shingles virus is known as Varicella zoster. It is a herpes virus but not the type that relates to cold sores. It doesn't relate to genital herpes, either. That one relates to a sexually-transmitted virus. Both of the noted herpes viruses relate to herpes simplex. Shingles relates to herpes zoster. Yet another herpes virus causes infectious mononucleosis, aka the kissing disease. There is yet another herpes virus that can kill in-utero babies. It is believed that the various herpes viruses, all total, cause more illnesses than any other virus grouping. Shingles is, very definitely, an illness. It is a disease, and diseases are illnesses. They make people ill.

The shingles virus is the type of virus that relates to having had chickenpox, when a person was younger. The body somehow contracted the chickenpox virus. In fact, sometimes after having the chickenpox, children come down with a case of shingles. Though shingles relates to chickenpox, it has nothing to do with chickens. Some primates may have harbored the virus, however, and still can, today; some have been noted with the chickenpox rash and pustules. Primates were also noted with monkeypox, in 1958 and at other times. The two are diseases not related. Monkeypox is a milder virus than smallpox. When monkeypox flares up in an area, they already know how to treat it. It can be contracted sexually or by contact. Cases of monkeypox occurred in eastern USA in 2022. It spread, especially among the gay community. The word, pox, refers to diseases that have a rash as a symptom (like smallpox and monkeypox). Monkeypox is an orthopox virus. An orthopox virus is a virus that affects both mammals and humans, like smallpox, cowpox, and horsepox. Like smallpox and cowpox, monkeypox relates to the variola virus, which is not the same virus that is related to chickenpox and shingles.

Early on, around 1796 and a little thereafter, Edward Jenner used actual cowpox in a vaccine to treat smallpox. He greatly contributed to establishing an immunology foundation, in the USA and the world. There was some modification of the smallpox vaccine over the years, but it was changed in 2008, when the African Green Monkey was used to establish the immunization.

Diseases that produce rashes aren't all related, and rashes can vary and be different. When I had shingles, there was no way I could consider the large pustules to be a rash, but some people put such pustules in the same arena as rashes. Rashes don't linger so long, and the virus that causes the more commonly described rash does not attach itself to nerves right under the skin, like the shingles virus does.

Chickenpox pustules or blisters are not as large as the shingles pustules are. They are scattered over the head and body, whereas shingles pustules or blisters are concentrated in one spot, or two spots (sometimes three)—all on one side of the body. Neither chickenpox nor shingles are all that dangerous, when compared to certain other diseases. In both cases, it is best to be quarantined until the blister or pustule crusts fall off. Chickenpox, itself, shows up as a rash, on the shoulders, neck, face, and scalp at first, but then it spreads over the body. It has left pit or pox marks on the skin of very few people. The lesions get infected by germs that happen to be around, too, and this can end out causing pits or scarring. Areas get scratched, because they can itch, and this can cause scarring but the rash and lesions can cause scarring, on their own. If left undisturbed, any liquid of the rash (or pustules, with some viruses) will absorb back into the skin. Chickenpos is chiefly a childhood disease. A sitz bath is sometimes helpful to relieve any itching, as is using calamine lotion but there is no cure and the virus is not killed. A sitz bath is a mixture of water and baking soda. Ask a physician about this bath, however, or a nurse, if you are in a hospital and feel you need a sitz bath. They are of general help relative to a number of ailments.

There is another disease associated with the shingles virus, Vericella-zoster, but there aren't usually any blisters or pustules, which seems odd. This disease is known as Ramsay Hunt Syndrome. Affected are facial nerves and especially those near the inner ear (on one side). It is an adult disease. The whole side of the face is affected. The virus attacks the nerves under the skin, which is what happens with shingles. The nerve damage can even go down around the ear drum. The patient has a puffed-out face (on one side) and cannot talk well because the tongue is affected, on one side. The patient can experience vertigo. Only about five out of a hundred thousand are affected by RHS per year so it is not too common. It takes a long time for the nerve pain to go away (like with the nerve pain with shingles). My guess is that stress causes this to flare up, and possibly excess sun exposure, but that is a guess and is best left to the medical profession to ascertain. With a chickenpox shot, when young, prevent

RHS? It is believed it will. Will a shingles shot, when advised by a physician, help to prevent RHS? Most likely it will but a physician must be consulted. People who are young should see a doctor about such shots, especially if they had chickenpox when they were young, but even if they didn't, they will want to get a shot to prevent chickenpox.

After a bout of chickenpox, it seems like the virus has gone away but it hasn't. It lives along a person's backbone very secretly, but it is not dead. It simply lives there and, even though it is a virus, it does not do anything damaging to the body as it continues to live inside it. It wreaks no havoc. It simply lives there for many years, and I do mean many. For example, if you had chickenpox at age eight and you get shingles at age sixty-eight, that would be sixty years that the shingles virus has been dormant. The whole time, there would be no signs or symptoms that you were a carrier and during this time, you will not transfer it to anyone else, which can be unusual for a virus (like the coronavirus (COVID), for example, which spreads like wildfire).

The shingles virus just secretly and quietly lives in the body for many years until something suddenly upsets it, usually after a person is around age fifty; it particularly gets agitated if people are in their seventies and even eighties but there are many recorded cases of people who were in their sixties and a little less so, and only in their fifties. Some get shingles when they are over ninety but fewer people are alive at that age so you would have to look at per-capita statistics (per head count) to know what the percentage index would be for that age group and as to how it would compare with other age groups. It would be somewhat high. All these age groups would not have had access to the chickenpox immunization, when they were young. It was not around when some and certain people were in school or were getting their shots, when they were very young.

When a person comes down with these unsightly shingles, the anti-viral medicine given for it does not kill the virus, which is the same situation you find with the dormant virus. Nothing can kill it. Sometime during the shingles flare-up, the virus goes back to the backbone area (or somewhere else), settles in there, and becomes dormant again. Some people think that it dies and goes away, but it cannot be killed . . . not as yet. They haven't come up with a drug to kill it, not even a sulfa drug. Sulfa drugs can kill some bacteria and some viruses. There are many sulfa drugs but they were dropped by the wayside because they became less used. They were a sulfanilamide based antibiotic used to destroy bacteria. They were replaced by better drugs.

Many drugs have been replaced by better drugs over the years. Synthetic bacteria-inhibiting drugs (any of the sulfa drugs) can be re-formatted to be made more effective. You have to wonder about drug re-formatting. It is likely a part of drug research. Sulfa drugs are many but they were taken over by penicillin. If someone builds up a tolerance to penicillin, a sulfa drug could possibly be used. What is used to arrest or kill bacteria likely won't work on a virus. Researchers may have tried some mixing and matching in labs but whatever gets done in labs has to be generally logical and within reason. Penicillin is a number of antibiotics—not just one—made using molds or made synthetically, to fight bacteria. Some people get bacteria-fighting drugs confused with virus-fighting drugs. It is easy to do.

Some people think that shingles relates to sexual transmission. They get it confused with one type of herpes that is transferred that way. Shingles has nothing to do with sexual transmission. You do not get shingles from having sex. Subconsciously, some people get this confused. You can get genital herpes from having sex, but shingles has nothing to do with genital herpes. Rash flare-ups are often chronic and at random times when a person has genital herpes. This varies from person to person. Medical researchers have been able to isolate similar and dissimilar viruses. Shingles has nothing to do with AIDS, either, though some people who already have AIDS can get shingles or that which looks like shingles because their immune system is way down in strength. They have to be carriers of the chickenpox virus, though, to have actual shingles.

Chickenpox and smallpox are totally different but people get them confused. Smallpox can be lethal. Smallpox can result in infection of the heart, lungs, and brain. Right before 1967, there were many, many deaths from smallpox—per year and world-wide. The vaccine started to be given out more widely in the USA, in 1967 and now, there are essentially no cases of smallpox. Stocks of the smallpox virus are kept at various disease-control centers around the world (or elsewhere). Certain countries have stocks, which will be needed in case of outbreaks. I do not know how these stocks are preserved. If they are supposed to be kept at a certain temperature, we had better be careful about Global Warming and about our power grids ever shutting down. Much that is medical will be ruined if electricity ever stops.

Smallpox has pustules that are infectious, like the chickenpox and shingles pustules are. They are many and they are small (unlike those of the chicken pox and shingles virus. With shingles, there is a contagious stage, as well, which means the patient should be under quarantine during the first part of the shingles ordeal. The very hour a person notices any of these large pustules on their body, they must quarantine themselves (after they go see the doctor first, and get all the medicine and medication they will need). There will be a conspicuous 'sick time' initially and the afflicted person will be under the weather and won't feel well because the virus is active and flaring up. The afflicted person will, actually, be ill. The person should take to bed and rest and convalesce. They should not be out and about in the public. They'll have a high temperature for a time and when the temperature breaks, then soon after that the virus will not be contagious but a shower will have to be taken, thereafter, before the person should mix with people.

Whereas this 'sick time' will not be too overwhelming, this is not the case with smallpox. You surely do get a conspicuous rash with smallpox. Smallpox will kill fast and spread easily (similar to the coronavirus or COVID). Like the coronavirus, smallpox will affect the respiratory tract so the lung areas are in jeopardy. All quarantine times for anyone with a contagious-disease must be learned and carefully observed. Smallpox is not 100% eradicated; historically, it has killed <u>millions</u>. It is well under control, now. Unfortunately, chickenpox and shingles are not yet eradicated. Again, if you had chickenpox (and some people don't remember if they did or didn't because they were so young), the Varicella-zoster virus will stay in your body.

Even though it lives along the backbone around the nerves there, you never feel anything there. Strangely, chickenpox does not cause the nerve damage that shingles sometimes does (i.e. the areas where the pustules were). You feel considerable nerve agitation (and even pain) in the area or areas where the shingles pustules show up. This is where all the pain comes in. They like nerves, usually one or more sensory nerves, at the nerve's trunk. They attach themselves to the nerves under where the pustules show up. This is why the pustules show up. Then, possibly because of the medicine you are given and that you end out taking for the shingles, it becomes motivated to go back to the backbone area to live.

Some bodies likely have more of the virus in them than other bodies have. To the degree that it can and does multiply is in the arena of medical research. It would 'appear' that because of its symptom patterns, it does not multiply, or multiply past a certain point. It may not be able to find ample location areas in the body to be able to comfortably live, but this would have to be confirmed by research specialists. The medicine taken at the beginning of the shingles ordeal forces the virus to do 'something' (like, re-locate), but again, the virus does not die because of the medicine. Are they trying to find a medicine that will go in and kill all of the virus:? Stay tuned. What about all the different kinds of steroids? Have they all been looked at? One can only hope that someone in some country will be able to discover such a drug.

Presently, there are no drugs that will kill this unwelcomed virus. It makes itself at home, once it enters. There is no actual cure for this virus or way to get rid of it for all time. All you can take for shingles, when they show up, is an anti-viral drug but again, no drug, yet known, can kill the virus. An anti-viral drug can only reduce complications while you have a shingles flare-up. Once the shingles episode is over, the shingles virus goes back to where it came from and continues to live there but some professionals think some of it could go to another area, as well. Wherever it goes, you don't feel it and there are no more pustules. The pustules you have dry up, but nerves near to where the pustules are become damaged and are very sore—for some time, too.

To clarify, when there is a shingles flare-up (and woe is you if you get them), the virus relocates itself and attacks the sensory nerves (at their trunk) in one or more areas of the body, causing inflammation and underlying nerve pain. Some more severe cases of shingles are treated with steroids (like cortisone). At some point in time, I was sure I should have had that treatment, but I never did have it. In retrospect, I'm glad I didn't. Taking any steroids can be problematic, with their side effects. There are some negatives on record about cortisone. These days, you have to research everything.

Some people have some kind of disease at the time when shingles' pustules show up on their body. Depending on the biological or neurological disease, there could be extra and even compounded complications because of the shingles flare-up so there will need to be more medical help. If somebody happens to have cancer, for example, and they get shingles, they could die so they must be under a doctor's care more consistently. Their immune system will be very weak, which is why they got the shingles in the first place. It is why anyone gets shingles but a weakened immune system can be, and is relative, as concerns different people

With shingles, you always get pustules or blisters, which are also called vesticles or pustules but I'll use the first two noted words, instead. Some people get a bad headache before the pustules show up, but that might not happen to everyone who gets shingles. Mainly, any time you feel sudden and unusual irritation and extreme sensitivity anywhere on your body, check out the area, topically. The pustules will be there. In other words, look at your skin in the area where the irritation or pain is. You can go for days, not knowing you have shingles pustules or blisters. I did. Even when you change your clothes, you may not see them, unless you happen to be standing in front of a mirror or happen to look down. Sometimes, a spouse or partner will see them before the person who has the shingles does. When anyone sees the shingles pustules, it can be startling and shocking.

You actually get the shingles days <u>before</u> the pustules or blisters show up and this can be important to know because the minute the pustules/blisters are detected is when the afflicted person must go in and get anti-viral medicine prescribed. Do not wait two or three days to go see a doctor. Go right away and that very day. It is actually an emergency. Do a walk-in if you can, at your Primary-Care physician's office. Tell them it is an emergency. The visit won't take long. All you have to do is show the doctor the affected area or areas and he'll see that you get an anti-viral prescription. Then, get the prescription filled right away (that very day), before you go home.

Medicine is different from medication. Medicine is what you take to kill germs or viruses, or at least curb them, alter their behavior, and retard or stop their growth. Medicine works alongside of the immune system. Medication is what you take to get rid of, or to relieve or reduce pain. Often, a patient will need to take both, or they'll want to take both but will only get the medicine prescribed. Opioids are pain relievers—medications. These are what doctors are nervous about these days—not, so much, the medicines. People form addictions to medications, but not, generally, to medicine. Think of a coin as having two sides. That coin would represent the world of prescription drugs (and when physicians want to be more cautious about when and what gets prescribed).

As a walk-in, explain to the desk receptionist at the doctor's office how important it is for you to be squeezed in, once you see the pustules. Wait in the reception room, if you have to. You have to get that anti-viral medicine as fast as possible. You can call first, too, and let them know how urgent it is for you to get the prescription. <u>You have a 72-hour window of opportunity before you start taking the medicine and if you miss that deadline, the treatment of the shingles may take longer and the case could end out being more severe.</u> <u>72 hours is three days.</u> <u>Time to get in to see a doctor is of the essence.</u> Again, this is an emergency. This is an actual disease you are dealing with. You must get in and get one or more prescriptions for it—especially one.

9

I was a little slow when getting to the doctor's with my shingles. It wasn't my fault. I did not see the pustules right away. If you end out with a more severe case, it will cause added stress because of the pain and the disruption to your life. For older people, the heart can even be affected when they have shingles. <u>It is actually a traumatic experience to get shingles</u>; the longer you have the neuralgia (or nerve pain), the more traumatic the experience will be. It is the neuralgia—the strong irritation <u>under</u> the skin and that stays around for a long time—that is very hard to contend with. The virus attacks the nerves under the skin. It wants to live around those nerves so it isn't an attack, per se. It attaches itself to nerves and that is what wreaks havoc, relative to the peace and calm of the afflicted person.

The shingles neuralgia I had, hung on so much longer than I was expecting it to. It affected me way more than I was first expecting, too. My daily life had many disruptions and interruptions, because of the neuralgia. These events included going to the doctor's, getting prescriptions filled, driving all over the place, getting behind in my work, experiencing the different pains and discomforts that shingles brought on, and undergoing continued and related sleep irregularities, which turned out to be very hard on me. I got behind on home chores, too, because I was not able to move around as much as usual due to the malaise and fatigue and the pains I was experiencing from any movement, especially when I was in bed.

When you get less sleep or less quality sleep, you need more sleep but less sleep becomes continual. No pillow in the world will help improve your sleep when you have shingles, which continues to affect you long after the pustules are gone. A good pillow may improve your sleep at other times, but it will not dull or remove nerve pain that tends to keep you awake. And yes, shingles are painful. They are not just irritating.

<u>Shingles are really awful because the affected area actually hurts.</u> Because of the nerve damage, you feel them no matter what you are doing and you feel them even when you are sitting down. They are especially terrible to contend with when you are lying down. When you have shingles, the less you move

around, the better, especially because there are certain painful areas and you usually don't just get one patch of shingles. Very often, you get at least two good-sized patches of them (or even more, sometimes). My two large areas were on both front and back, which was bad. A few people only get one patch, so the shingles experience is easier on them.

I first started feeling the shingles' pain along my right rib area, to one side of my chest, and also on my back area, which was straight across from and through to that front area (only it was in the back). Both were on my right side. I first thought it was my gallbladder that I was feeling and that either I'd passed a gallstone with some difficulty so there was a residual pain (and that this was what the pain was from), or that I was in process of passing a gallstone. The area where the pain was, was right about where the gallbladder is, and I'd had a huge bout with passing a gallstone a couple of years earlier so I naturally assumed that this incident was another gallstone incident, even though it seemed a little different. The pain in back, that matched the location of the pain in front (only it was in the back), I assumed was related to the same gallstone issue. I reasoned, well what else could it be? And nothing else came to mind.

I assumed the pain would go away and I essentially assumed that I'd already passed the stone because the related pain seemed to be less even though pain was still present from the irritation to the passageway that the gallstone would have travelled through, especially when you consider that there are curves or corners along the passageway that the gallstone could have somewhat harmed, as it was travelling through.

Having a gallstone and passing a gallstone can be much more pain than shingles is. If the stone gets constricted, in any way and anywhere, that pain will be horrendous and almost indescribable. Sometimes, when a gallstone that is longer lasting gets passed, there was likely obstructing along the way. The gallstone can get stuck in the passageway. It can still get through but it may not get through right away. You feel pain all over the torso, in both front and back, when you have such a gallstone. With my first-passed gallstone, the pain eventually went away but that was after I was medically seen at a hospital and treated and given lots of antibiotics, as well as some morphine. (Thank the Lord for morphine.) I was told I'd passed the gallstone immediately before the area was looked at (but after I'd arrived at the hospital) but again, much pain was still there. It leaves some pain, even after it passes. It left a very pained area in its wake. It didn't even feel like I'd passed it, but I had.

I believe the rogue gallstone had done some kind of temporary damage along the way, as it travelled, and I was lucky the damage was not permanent. It slowly and gradually healed up after I left the hospital but it took a while. I was aware of some pain but I did not request any additional painkillers, at the time. That's the way I am. Just the ones they gave me at the hospital were all I used. I do not believe in taking more painkillers than are absolutely necessary. The pain wasn't that hard to tolerate. The stone has passed.

It took some time for the residual pain from the gallstone incident to completely go away, but it did (and I was glad I chose to not have my gallbladder removed because that subject had come up and I did not want them to take it out. It was my first gallstone.). At the time, I had many stray cats around my home. They were outside and needing to be fed, and fast, because I'd already been in the hospital a few days and desperately wanted to get back home to take care of them. My indoor cats had plenty of food and water (I was able to see to that before I left, strange as that may seem, and I'd even driven myself to the hospital, which, to me and in retrospect, seems even stranger but you do what you have to do and I was able to do this because I concentrated intensely on my driving and was forced to ignore my pain). There were no cars on the road. It was in the middle of the night when the pain had hit me.

With the shingles pain, I continued to feel the pain all night long but I thought that it had been caused by a gallstone, I thought I'd just wait it out and believed the pain would go away, in time, because the gallstone had passed (but it wasn't really a gallstone, it was really shingles). I, unfortunately, waited longer than I wish I had before I went to see my Primary-Care physician because I assumed what I assumed and that the pain was from a gallstone and the gallstone had passed so everything was all-right. Not too much longer after the pain came on, I needed to shower. That is when I first saw the two large patches of pustules. I saw the front one first. I felt the one on the back with my hand and then saw the area, in a mirror. The papule areas were really what had been causing the pain—this, I very quickly knew.

How my mouth dropped when I saw the set of two ugly papule groups! As noted before, very ugly areas were in front, over the top rib area on the right side and under my right breast and they were also over and around on my back, in that somewhat adjacent area to the front area where the front spots were (and on my right side). I was certainly not expecting to see such ugly sites. They were scary. I had no clue what they were, or why they were.

The spots or sores looked like a rash from a distance, but not up close. A rash has tiny blisters, or no blisters at all and is just reddish-colored bumps. Most rashes itch, and strangely, the pustule areas did not itch, at least, not too much. I couldn't have scratched them anyway, even if there was any itching because the whole area was so bumpy and raw feeling. The area under the pustules was raw, and open, except for the covering of the pustules. The pustules hurt, instead of itching. You wouldn't think that one or two areas of huge-sized blisters would hurt, but believe me, they did. Words cannot relay . . . . The attacks on the nerves actually expanded out a little under the skin and around from where the blisters were, quite frankly, so the pain covered a larger area than an observing outsider would have thought it did. Of course, the afflicted person knows the truth.

The large blisters or pustules were all concentrated in the two areas and they were pretty ugly, which caused my mouth to drop even further when I first laid eyes on them. I couldn't even imagine what they were, or what was going on. Talk about panic! I'd never even known anyone who had had shingles. I'd never learned anything about shingles. It was all in the unknown realm, to me. I'd heard the word, but that is about it.

The areas were so different from general rash areas, which we all get from time to time, and bumps are many but they are tiny. These were large pustules and they were packed with fluid. Some of them were bigger than you'd think they'd be—but they were all sizes, really. I hesitate to call them blisters because the pustules are much bigger than blisters are, but I suppose they can be called blisters because they rise up so much and because of the fluid. At first this fluid is a clear liquid but it will soon turn cloudy. They're just really rather large blisters. I tend to think of blisters as being solo, not all in a group—like, a blister you would get on a foot from wearing a too-tight shoe. I surely was not expecting to see this disturbing sight on either my front or my back area and, of course, I panicked. You probably would have, too. I mean, what were these skin invasions? I'd never even seen anything close to looking like them—on anyone else, and definitely on me. They take a while to dry up, too, so you are stuck with them from a week to ten days.

My son looked up my doctor's hours for me on his computer and I went in that next morning (after my night of horror) and they were able to work me in. (My doctor is always booked.) My condition was diagnosed as shingles and again, I had really known nothing about them. My mind had been going all over the place, thinking that I had some kind of horrible disease.

Apparently, since I'd had chickenpox as a child and never got the chickenpox vaccination before I got them, I had been harboring this virus in my body for years (and since I was a child). I do not recall getting actual shingles right after the chickenpox bout. I only remember the chickenpox. My immune system had been low when I got the shingles and I'd been stressed and so the virus reacted and the shingles was activated and decided to show up. Again, shingles tend to come out in older people (after age fifty) and I was definitely over age fifty. Something seems to trigger their movement and activity. There could be heat exposure, vitamin deficiency, a cold or the flu, not getting enough sleeps, acute stress, and even being overly active. There could be any combination of these, as well. Shingles can be a one-time flare-up but on rare occasion, there can be another flare-up after the first one, later on, but it is usually very mild. Don't ask me why. I simply don't know . . . and do doctors even really know why that is? Some could, I suppose. I think it is all very strange.

I was glad to learn there was a chance for there to only be one more (very mild) flare-up, if even that, because as it turned out, the shingles I had this first time gradually become very painful and the case lasted way too long. I certainly did not want to get them a second time, after the first episode, but if I ever do get them now, again, even without my having a shingles shot, the second bout is supposed to be much milder than the first bout had been. Again, I find this to be strange, because as you get even older, your immune system is apt to weaken even more.

At least with my particular case of shingles, outsiders could not see them. My clothes covered them up. Some people get them on a lower leg or arm, so they are seen, then. Some will, sadly, get them on their face. No one can miss seeing those. They're unsightly, and people balk when they notice them on someone.

Though there are other anti-virus medicines for shingles, I was prescribed Valacyclovir 9, aka Valtrex®. I was to take it for at least seven days but I had a second prescription filled and took it for an extra three days. Subconsciously, I thought that since I likely didn't start taking it within 72 hours of the shingles showing up that I needed to take it for a few more days and so, right or wrong, that is what I did and why I took the medicine for ten days, instead of seven.

This noted medicine is not anti-bacterial, like antibiotics tend to be. It is anti-viral. Antibiotics tend to kill bacterial germs. Anti-viral medicine kills viruses. There are probably more antibiotics out than anti-virals. Medicine will be bacteria or virus-specific and will combat the specific bacteria, or virus. One anti-viral medicine does not kill all viruses or hold all of them back. Each virus invasion is virus-specific and needs virus-specific medicine. AIDS is also a viral disease and the virus is, often, not killed by certain anti-viral medicines. They have come up with some successful anti-viral medicines and shots for AIDS but it took a while. A virus seems to be tougher to kill or get rid of than bacterium (but there can be exceptions). Remember, not all viruses are killed or will die. Viruses have a coating and so they are hard to penetrate. Bacterium and microbes are more exposed and out in the open (to the effects of the medicine). They have no coating around them. That is the general difference but there is so much more to this overall subject that it requires considerable scholastic study.

If an immunity to an antibiotic medicine is built up in a person's body, all bacterial germs will not always be killed by the antibiotic. An antibiotic can lose effect because someone can build up an intolerance to it. If a viral medicine does not kill a virus, it may have nothing to do with tolerance build-up. The virus just can't be killed. With certain viruses, nothing seems to kill them . . . so far. We live in a dangerous world. There's been SARS (Severe Acute Respiratory Syndrome) and MERS (Middle-East Respiratory Syndrome) and different strains of coronavirus or COVID, among others.

Viruses pass from animals to humans, but not every virus an animal can have will jump to humans. Some may be passed but won't affect humans. Some viruses may only affect some humans. Others will affect all humans. Certain animals are more prone to having certain viruses. For example, some people believe the COVID-19 started off with bats. Animals we have, more particularly, known to have been prone to carrying a virus are actually few. The world of viruses is unseen but where there is life, there will be viruses. Viruses need moisture. They live in blood. They live in body linings that are moist. Put in an all-dry area and they will die—fast or more slowly, but they will die. Bacteria dies in an all-dry area, too. Living germs do not like 'dry'. When dry, they die.

Early on, someone told me to drink lots of water. I do not know if that had anything to do with taking the Valacylovir 9 and the drinking lots of water was because of that, or if it was good to drink lots of water because of the shingles virus and because of the illness that comes about from having shingles. I suspect the 'drinking water' idea was because of the medicine. When anyone has a high temperature, they become dehydrated because they perspire more, and so, they must drink more water. I know my temperature was higher for some time because of the shingles. When a temperature is not normal, people need more fluids because of perspiration and the moisture they keep on losing, which can vary along the way. It is never good to get dehydrated. People don't even know when they are dehydrated. Some medicine can increase your temperature, too, and so people will need more fluids for that reason, as well. Some medicine can be a little rough to have to take and we all know about side effects. Some can be bad. Sometimes there are multiple side effects. Fortunately, most side effects may not last that long—twenty-four to forty-eight hours, in the main, but it all depends on the medicine or medication. Some will last longer. Some last as long as you take the pills.

Because my doctor was skittish about prescribing opioids for painkillers (like a milder form of morphine, perhaps), another shingles medication known as Gabapentin was prescribed for shingles and it was prescribed rather often by him. Gabapentin is not really a pain reliever, though. It is just a nerve-pain inhibitor (not a nerve-pain reliever). I was also prescribed Tylenol® 500, and it really was of little help. It did not take the pain away. This is not because it is not a good product. It works well for some kinds of milder pain, it just wasn't strong enough to rid me of my shingles-related pain. Tylenol® 500 works well for headaches, possibly some muscle pain, and it reduces other kinds of pain.

The pain I constantly felt got worse, too, but it was especially bad whenever I tried to lie down. I couldn't rest or sleep on my right side, for absolute positive sure and for quite a long time. The very thought of it (later on) made me cringe—just the very memory of it. The nerve pain extended to the one side area (on the right) because of the shingles in the front and the shingles in the back. The pain was all along where the shingles were and the nerve damage seemed to radiate outward, some, from those sites, and so the nerve damage went around to that whole one side of my body. The nerve pain (or neuralgia), area-wise, was about six inches wide and long all the way around. Both patches were roundular but not all shingles patches are roundular. Some are oblong. Some are totally irregular-shaped, like an ink spot is. The pustule patch was not too far up from the waist, in both the front and back. This shingles pattern is somewhat common.

<u>Shingles only affects one side of the body and never the other side at the same time and that is one way you can know that the liquid-filled pustules or blisters are shingles.</u> The shingles pustules cover the affected areas and there is nerve damage and pain under that area but again, the nerve damage and pain actually extends outward a little from where the pustules are. So, again, the nerve pain, from start to finish, includes a larger area than onlookers (who observe the patch of pustules or blisters) might think. The person who has the shingles knows, though, because they're the ones living with the nerve damage, hour by hour by hour.

I know there are lotions or creams a person can put on the shingles pustules but I had heard (right or wrong) that they didn't have much effect. Besides, I did not want to touch the pustules and you have to touch them when you put on the cream or lotion. My doctor emphasized that you must not touch the blisters. <u>The liquid in the pustules is highly contagious and if an outsider were to touch the liquid, they could get chickenpox.</u> The pustules generally do not break open. They are really thick. The liquid disappears as the pustules dry up so assumedly, the liquid seeps or soaks into the body. I assume that is what happened with mine (but I wasn't paying that close attention to them as they were always covered by clothes). Also, I really didn't want to look at them—they were so ugly. Some of them might break open, though. I do not recall this happening with me, though, not even once. I ended out wondering if a medical professional were to lance the blisters, then, if the liquid didn't go back into the body, because it had been lanced and manually sponged and dried off, would there, then, be less of the virus going back into the body? Unfortunately, I couldn't find anything out about that on the Internet. It's just an interesting question to ponder. Only actual medical research people are apt to know of any lancing versus not lancing outcomes and benefits.

I was tempted to lance the front blisters myself (I couldn't see the back ones to be able to do that), but I remembered how contagious the liquid was, so, being spooked about that, even though I'd already had chickenpox, I left them alone. I did not want to re-infect or additionally infect myself. Sure enough, after ten days, the liquid in the blisters had dried up and/or gone back into my body. I do not recall even a one of them breaking open on their own, but any of them could have, I suppose. I think I would have known it if they had, though. I would have felt the liquid.

When I showered, I washed the pustules areas with soap that I'd lathered on the flat of my hand. I did not want to use anything harsh on the areas, like a brush or even a washcloth. Any of them could have opened up and drained while I was showering, though. I'm just not aware that any did. Honestly, I just don't know what happened to the liquid. Retrospectively, that seems strange. I know the dried-up pustules become brownish, which related to blood drying. Initially, the pustules were a clear liquid, then became cloudy, a little, but when they dried, they were brownish underneath. As I did not like looking at them, I didn't pay real close attention to them. I do not know when or specifically how they turned brownish.

Sleeping became extremely difficult because I kept waking up. No matter how I slept, there was pain. To emphasize, there were several areas where the nerve damage was extremely painful. Also, these areas would act up, on occasion, even when I was sitting and moving very little. There would be occasional throbbing pain, too—like the virus was hitting one particular inside area with a hammer. Those were no fun to have to experience. In some areas where all the nerve damage was (which was under but also around where the pustules showed or had showed), there would be a burning feeling. One spot on my back would suddenly feel like a six-inch by six-inch area that was being burned with a chemical. Virus gremlins would attack that area. I'd never know when the throbbing or the burning pain would come about or act up, but it was awful whenever it did.

In addition to this under-the-skin neuralgia, the upper area over where the nerve damage was had that burning feeling. It was much worse at the start of the shingles ordeal. It was somewhat like a topical steam burn that you would feel on your skin. It was an open sore area on top of the skin that took time to heal. It got a little better—slowly. The burning feeling was still around, topically, after many weeks and so were those unpredictable, off-and-on pain waves, under the surface of the skin and in both the front and back areas. They never seemed to leave me alone. They would hit me at random times. They'd get me when I sat or when I rested and slept. I do not know why this off and on hammering and throbbing pain would occur. It seems strange, though. It didn't seem to be caused by anything in particular. Body movement, even slight, could have had something to do with it, but I can't swear to that. I just know that for some time, there was that kind of pain at the two shingles sites.

I was able to sleep on the left side only. I absolutely could not move to my front, back, or other side or it would be making the nerve damage areas worse and cause even worse pain. It felt like all the little nerves were super-inflamed after I had laid down on any one of those areas. It just didn't work. For the longest time, I ended out sleeping for three or four hours, at most, on my left side only; then I'd wake up. Sometimes I'd sleep less. I'd get more tired more easily, too, because of the 24/7 strain. My whole schedule was thrown way off and that was hard on me psychologically because I had a number of books I was trying to finish, all at the same time, and I wanted to plough through and get them done but the shingles really ended out setting me back and I was only able to work one-third the time or at most, one-half the time that I usually worked because of my sleep problems and the shingles ordeal. I'd get so worn down and was tired when I was awake, quite often, and sleep problems, weakness, and change in routine are all notorious symptoms and causes of the shingles. Plus, lethargy and fatigue are the side effects of the anti-viral medicine so I was between a rock and a hard place, all across the board.

I couldn't escape my constantly being tired. It was hell, quite frankly. Remember, I am an older woman to begin with, too, and also, I have a medical disorder because my stomach is up in my chest pressing against my lungs so I have less breathing capacity and get a little less oxygen than other people do, which means, I become a little more tired than usual. So, I'd get a little tired because of that, a little tired from the shingles, and a little tired from the shingles medicine. It was not so easy going.

I'd gone in and insisted on a stronger pain medication than the Tylenol® 500 and my doctor would not prescribe an opioid. I didn't really ask him to, not specifically, and maybe I should have but he did prescribe that nerve-pain inhibitor—Gabapentin®—and it was a twice-a-day medicine but after just three or four hours, I'd feel the pain come back but could not take another pill for another eight or nine hours. Again, it was not a bona fide painkiller. Some medication gets prescribed, these days, which only somewhat reduces pain but it does not really relieve pain and make it not be felt. I finally figured out that I needed to take one of those Gabopentin® pills right before I was about to go to sleep, especially at night. That way, I'd sleep a little longer at night, and this happened, and so this helped me to get back on my schedule a little better, but only somewhat because I would still get tired after about four hours, once I woke up.

Again, the medicine made me tired. Again, too, the nerve damage and related pain also made me tired. It was a vicious cycle I was caught up in. I'm trying to be as specific as I can when remembering details and the sequence of the ordeal. Possibly, the shingles got to me more because of my medical disorder (i.e. my stomach pressing in against my lungs). Pain always makes people tired, and again, lethargy and fatigue were side effects of the nerve-pain reduction pills, which really did not help with the pain all that much and I soon stopped taking those pills. They really weren't that much help—not in my case. I would have preferred a low dosage opioid. Painkillers can add to your fatigue, though. They can make you dopey and sluggish.

Still and all, my sleep would be interrupted after about four or five hours for some time so I'd get up and work for however long I was able to work before I would get sleepy again and then I'd go and try to sleep again but sometimes, I couldn't sleep because of the pain so I'd watch some TV while I was in bed. I ended out seeing some interesting middle-of-the-night programs and some of them were really good, thankfully. I kept the volume down pretty low. Eventually, I'd drop off to sleep with the TV still on (not good but it was unavoidable). I'd keep thinking I would fall asleep while I was laying there and sometimes, I just didn't. At times, I'd doze off for a while, wake up not long afterwards, and start working again. This new pattern of existence (sleeping fewer hours) got established and I lived that way for some time because the neuralgia stayed around for quite a long time. It became quite the foe. It was stuck on me, like a bunch of leeches.

PART 2
Early concerns, inconveniences, and prescription drugs

<u>Early on, I read that it could take several months before the nerve endings healed and that some people can even have the neuralgia for up to a year.</u> What was meant by 'several months', I would soon discover. My suspicion was that some of the nerve endings would heal up faster than others and that some pain areas and spots would take longer to stop menacing me. My doctor had told me the shingles would be gone in a couple of weeks. That statement gave me some hope. At the same time, I assumed he was talking about the pustules <u>and</u> the pain, but in retrospect, I have to conclude that he was only talking about the pustules and not the neuralgia because the neuralgia hung on for many months. It was all very grueling. Grinning and bearing was not so easy to do.

Neuralgia is one of those euphemistic, soft-sounding words so it is not all that descriptive of what neuralgia really is. It's kind of like the word, died. Passed-away is a less harsh word (a euphemism) than the word, died. And on the subject of death, there have been people who have died or passed away because of shingles, especially older people, and also, again, even people in their nineties have been set back by shingles. The older a person gets, they are more apt to have certain medical issues and shingles can complicate those medical issues.

As previously noted, shingles tends to hit older people and these older people most likely have compromised immune systems and a greater chance of dying when shingles hits. In this respect, this virus has similarity to the coronavirus (COVID). Odds are much greater that an older person will die, with the coronavirus. Shingles is less dangerous than COVID-19 (and its variants or sub-variants). Shingles can affect your blood pressure. Older people may be taking medication for something, too, and it may be problematic for them to combine meds (i.e. any shingles meds with whatever other med or meds they are taking). Early on, there were some meds being used for COVID-19 but they weren't, yet, being mass distributed. Early on in the coronavirus quarantine, there were three vaccinations brought forward

During the start of COVID, there were the three vaccinations available in the USA all of which were controversial as they hadn't gone through enough formal testing. Many elderly people died from the coronavirus but the disease got younger people, too. The elderly were the most vulnerable. The vaccinations proved to be reliable. One was discontinued, after a time. A large number of people were afraid of having any of them. They seemed to work with any subsequent variants, too, though there could have been some altering with the vaccinations to make them more effective against the different strains or mutations (variants). When someone got COVID, it was hard to know what variant they had, or if they had the original COVID-19. Some people thought that the noted variants were really COVID-19 and that the government just wanted people to think there were variants because conquering COVID-19 had not been so easy and was going so slow. That is being a little too suspicious, for me. Some viruses seem to mutate or alter. Others do not. Why and how any of them do is mysterious. Boosters came out after the series vaccinations had been out for a while. It was noted, by some health professionals, that people should get a COVID booster once a year, like they would a flu shot. Some were skittish about doing that but many weren't. Governments paid for the series vaccinations and for a couple of the boosters (for those who had them in sequence). COVID subsided but by early 2023, had there been herd immunity? Many say no, not quite. If COVID builds up again, governments would keep paying for any vaccinations, one would assume. Some feel there are more vaccinations that the different governments should pay for, which relate to prevention of other diseases or viral attacks. This would include chickenpox, and shingles shots. It is really unfortunate that so many people get shingles and that so many children did not get vaccinated for chickenpox. There should be certain universal immunizations.

Even finding a med that could slow down the viral growth and attacks so the body's immune system would have more time to fight off the virus would have prevented many deaths. Sometimes, this is all that can be done with certain viruses until a better vaccine comes along. Such a remedy medicine could save many lives, but not all lives. It has to be at-the-ready, constantly, and in all places, and therein is the problem, too—immediate access to a remedy or partial remedy that can hold back the invading virus so the body has time to fight it as it tries to take over. A partial remedy is better than no remedy. It can give the immune system a chance to fight the virus better, and to therefore prevail over the virus and save a life. Of course, it is a vaccine that is needed, along with that which holds a virus back after the person already has been attacked by the virus. There is a vaccination, before contracting a virus, and medicine that can hold it back when someone already has the virus.

A vaccine is essentially the same as an immunization. The words are synonymous. The word, immunization, somewhat implies that the contents given will fully immunize and make immune, and sometimes the contents that go into a person will make immune, but not always. With COVID, the contents given do not make totally immune. The person vaccinated can still get COVID, be contagious, and have symptoms but those symptoms will probably be significantly less acute. They may even be really mild. Once immunized or vaccinated, the person is not apt to die from COVID. They aren't totally immune, though, which is why some people prefer the word, vaccination versus immunization. Either word can be used, though. You are immunized to a large degree (but not completely) if you have and keep up with COVID anti-viral shots. Not many immunizations are given in oral form; most are given via a needle going in to the arm or buttocks. It was easier (and less personal) to give COVID shots in the arm. There didn't seem to be much option. The shots were given so quickly and people often had to line up, keeping a six-foot distance from everyone else. There is also the word, inoculation, which means that a serum or antibody is introduced into an organism so that a disease can be treated or prevented. You inoculate a person with a vaccine so that they will be immunized.

Russia came out with a partial remedy for COVID in July of 2020. France and China began to use partial-remedy treatment a little sooner, as well. The USA tried partial-remedy treatment, but only up to a point, during that first summer of COVID-19 (in 2020). Partial remedy at least gave some people hope and kept some people alive. If someone got COVID-19, there would at least be a partial treatment (a hold-back) that would give that person some hope, assuming the person would end out getting ahold of it, because not everybody could). Soon (around the early part of 2021), immunizations for the coronavirus came out and began to be distributed. There were three main ones, but several others were being distributed around the world, as well. Two required two doses (the Pfeizer and the Moderna), and one required one dose (the Johnson and Johnson). New strains or variants of COVID-19 were developing, but they were being managed. Some people opted to not have any of the immunizations because they believed more in specific medicines (after you got COVID) that weren't really specified for COVID use but that they genuinely thought would work. Two, in particular, were being used by some physicians (and likely still are)—Ivermectin and Remdesivir. Regardless of some of this thinking, more and more people went with the vaccinations the government was approving. Governments around the world paid for mass vaccinating. Another medicine came about for COVID treatment a little later—Paxlovid. Some pharmacies were able to dispense it without a prescription if someone had medical papers indicating they needed it. Will these lab specialists and researchers come up with something better for shingles? It is amazing when you think about how many vaccines are made up for school children and people in general year after year after year, but new vaccines and improved vaccines need to come out, too.

Some people ended out getting only one immunization versus the two, when they were supposed to have two doses. The one dose helped, but only up to a point. One type of the shingles immunization requires two doses. The first dose is only preventative, up to a point. The second and final dose has to be received within a certain period of time and provides more conclusive prevention (from death). After a time, booster immunizations came on the scene. Like with the polio vaccine, and the smallpox vaccine, people are hoping better immunizations will come out concerning all strains of COVID. Treatment is another area that has not had fast improvement. Not all places treat COVID the same way. Some seemed to have had better success. Improved treatment is what people are hoping for.

COVID-related vaccines (and boosters) came out quickly (from 2020 to 2023), for adults, teenagers, young children, and infants—in that order. They were lauded and accepted, but some people resisted them and even rejected them. The COVID vaccines became politicized. Other immunizations, when they came out, were likely well received by most everybody. They weren't politicized. For years, people were laid back about politics, for the most part. Politics has polarized many people, but it is really all about money the government gets and where is it going to go and who is it going to go to. All logic aside, people just want as much as they can get, for themselves or for their group. They can get blinded and aren't able to see a bigger picture. Logic not being aside, most all reserves are going to have to go towards Global Warming remedy now, including natural disaster relief as it keeps building up. Money for that needs to always be in reserve and people have to scramble more to find whatever work they can. People are going to have to learn to do without or live on less. People can't be expecting charity and extended welfare because natural disasters . . . and wars . . . are coming down the pike. Immigration is getting to be too costly. Welfare is overly distributed and is getting obese. The space program is getting to be too costly. Food and commodity needs some price increasing restrictions and price restrictions should be in place all over the nation, and the world. You would hope it would all be voluntary, but it won't be. More money needs to go into public health. Many more vaccinations should be free, than are, all around the world. More workers are needed in the field (in all areas).

Shingles is presently more of a senior citizen disease or ailment, whether the afflicted person is a junior, intermediate, or senior, senior citizen. A junior, senior citizen goes from around fifty-five to sixty-five. An intermediate, senior citizen goes from around sixty-five to seventy-five, and a senior, senior citizen goes from around seventy-five to a hundred. After a hundred they are a supra-senior, senior citizen. Again, anyone past fifty is vulnerable to getting a shingles attack, which is really what it is—an attack.

My shingles were all too interruptive. It must be hard for those who have to work a 9 to 5 job to have to cope with shingles. I work out of my home so I can rest and sleep when it strikes me to do so. I'm really somewhat of a workaholic (since 1998 when I started to write full-steam ahead). I try to keep a balance in my life, and I am usually a very early riser, but all that changed when I got shingles. My sleeping became disgustingly erratic. At least at home I don't have to look my best. I can go casual and even be a little sloppy when I'm in my home. When I had the shingles, I did not look my best. At times, I probably looked my worst.

As previously noted, some people don't get a real bad case of shingles. They may get them in one area and may only get a few pustules. Mine were really in the three already-noted areas—the front, back, and the neuralgia extended over to the right side so I'm counting in the side area as an area, as well. Because one patch of pustules was right below my right breast and the nerves were attacked all the way around to the side area and then, another patch was over to the back, I guess you can say my shingles case was more full-blown than other shingles cases may have been. I don't think the term, full-blown, is ever used in connection with shingles, though. (That would be a question for a doctor, though.) Full-blown is used when describing AIDS. Is it used to describe other ailments? Probably, yes.

There are many places where shingles can appear, but again, it's always on one side of the body and they are not only above the waist. They can almost be anywhere. Most of the pictures I saw of them were all above the waist but I know they can be anywhere on the body. I saw a few pictures that showed shingles on legs and feet. Some have gotten shingles around the mouth and in the mouth. Some unfortunates have gotten them around the eye area, which is very dangerous and can somehow cause blindness. Just exactly how, a medical specialist would know. I suspect this could relate to the liquid in the pustules and maybe, to the nerve damage the virus causes, but I surely do not know and anyone with the pustules around the eyes must seek quick medical help. Special treatment and prescriptions will be needed. Very young people have even gotten shingles around their eyes.

Shingles always come in patches. When the virus can become a patch, it will, because it has the space to become a patch. If there is room for the virus to form in a round shape, it will be a round patch, like on the back area or on the front chest area. It is more common to get a rounded patch of blisters on both the chest and the back at the same time (which, as a reminder, always makes it very hard to sleep). Women can sometimes get them under the breast area, over the ribs. They can get them anywhere on the chest. Men get them in the same general areas as women do.

To emphasize, even though they only show up on one side of the body, there will often be two or more patches. Two is the more common. Less common is when just one patch shows up. Shingles can show up on the face, the neck, the hand, a finger, the upper and lower arm, the stomach, the upper and lower leg, and not so often, around the feet. I'm not so sure it likes the more fatty areas, where bone is not close to. It shows up more where bones are close to the skin, but again, it is the sensory nerves it is after, wherever it can find any. In other words, shingles can pretty much show up anywhere on the body and if pustules or blisters are ever seen, anywhere, get to the doctor's, fast.

So often, people who get shingles don't even know what they are, let alone why the shingles go to where they go. They are very upset when they see them. Because the virus attaches to the nerve endings and is not just topical, as a rash would be, it takes quite a long time for shingles to heal. The virus damages the nerve endings and you hope that all the damaged nerves will heal up and that they'll heal up sooner rather than later and you assume that it will heal up quickly but it doesn't. Every day that goes by, you really do not know how long the pain will last and this lack of knowing can be tormenting. You may not realize that healing could take months, but it does.

Sadly, the healing of shingles goes <u>really</u> slow. You become more than aware of this, every day. For however long you end out having the neuralgia will be however long you will need the nerve-pain reduction pills (the Gabopentin®) or something similar because there are more than one type of prescribed medicine that is available for shingles). To emphasize, these pills are not pain-reliving pills, they are pain-reduction pills and they did not help me with all that much. The Gabopentin® may work well with others and may be effective in certain situations but to again emphasize, I would have been happier with something stronger, like a milder opioid drug, assuming they're useable alongside of something that is viral. I don't know what the different pain-relief options were that my doctor had but I never got to find out. I got through the ordeal, but could it have been easier on me if I'd had actual painkillers, especially early on? Yes, it would have been.

As noted earlier, if you catch the virus early and start taking the Valacyclovir 9 (or another anti-viral medicine) before 72 hours has elapsed, the length of time you have the shingles, and the severity of the shingles, will be less. Other countries may handle shingles cases differently. Another anti-viral medicine is Aciclover. Some shingles patients are prescribed that. It would be good to ask your doctor about idoxuridine and vidarabine, too, if you ever get shingles around your eyes. If the virus goes for the eye, the condition is known as dendritic keratitis and it can scar the cornea. Herpetic infections of the eye will require special and extra care.

Again, and to emphasize, it is important to recognize shingles for what they are, immediately, and to get the anti-viral medicine that very day or, at least, the next day. Because they were covered by my clothes and I did not see them, I did not get in as fast as I should have and was a little over the cusp, so to speak, so probably, in the back of my mind and along the way, I suspected that my shingles case was going to heal up over a longer period of time, which is exactly what happened but I could not help the delay because I did not know I even had the pustules. One reason why I'm writing the book is to put others on alert, should they ever get any shingles pustules.

As you are supposed to start taking the anti-viral medicine before 72 hours have elapsed, you have that period of time (three days) to get it or the case will be more acute. To anyone who ever gets shingles (I'm going to note it again), be warned. Get to the doctor's. Get the medicine. Presently and as I am writing this, I have no clue how long I'll have the nerve pain, aggravation, and related distractions, which is exactly what they are. You think about them all the time. The nerve pain reminds you to think about them. Again, I don't blame myself because I got in late. It's just one of those things. This has happened to many other people. Some people keep working and don't go see the doctor. Some people don't have medical insurance and don't go see the doctor.

As noted before, I wasn't happy with the pain medication (the Tylenol® 500 was too weak), so I eventually just stopped taking it. It was also an over-the-counter medication, in the area where the aspirins were. Some pharmacies won't dispense it even when there is a prescription for it because it is available over-the-counter. Likely, only certain pain medication fits well with what is viral as opposed to with what is bacterial, once something flares-up in the body. You never want a pain medication that reduces the effect of any anti-viral medicine. Doctors know about strengths, combinations, different prescriptions, and all these issues, when they go to prescribe anything.

Itching started up after the pustules were gone. Any itching is off and on, but, again, you can't scratch anywhere because it is very painful to press down on the nerve-damaged areas in any way, including just slightly. If you irritate those areas, it feels like pins and needles, somewhat, so you quickly stop, or if you are lying down and irritating the area, that is no fun, either, and so you have to re-position yourself. Anytime you accidentally put pressure on a nerve-pain area, you have to stop whatever it is you are doing and re-shift your position.

Initially, there is a fever, because of the virus. You may not notice it but you won't feel good, because of it. Off and on there can be a fever, too, somewhat because of the medicine and medication. I didn't take the anti-viral and the nerve-pain reducing meds at the same time (i.e. exactly concurrently). I was taking the anti-viral one with the Tylenol® 500 at the same time, initially and for a while. I only got the nerve-pain reducing medicine after I'd finished with the anti-viral one, which was after the previously-noted ten days. Even though doctors don't always prescribe the same medicine for shingles, you might be able to ask the doctor to prescribe a specific medicine, if you know of any good ones. You can also ask for a painkiller, if your shingles case is a bad one. It's worth a try. Why my doctor would not prescribe a mild opioid, at least initially and for a time, is not clear to me, but the opioid crisis had been going on and many doctors had become hyper-sensitive about prescribing them.

Antibiotics are not used against shingles. What is anti-viral is used, and there's a difference. Antibiotics involve the chemical altering of that which is produced by a micro-organism (like bacteria or fungi). The antibiotics are made with a diluted amount and they are able to go in and kill or to at least inhibit certain micro-organisms in different ways. They're quite miraculous, all across the board. More keeps being learned in the antibiotics field.

Different kinds of penicillin will kill bacteria strains and inhibit their growth but the non-active bacteria in a resting stage don't die so more than one dosage of penicillin is needed. It is an antibiotic and a wonder drug. Actively growing and reproducing bacteria die, because of penicillin. A patient can build up a resistance to antibiotics. Many diseases have a rash as a symptom and they all need antibiotics, but shingles does not really cause a rash, it causes pustules. Liquid is inside large pustules and they are not that small. A rash is composed of tiny bumps, not large pustules. There are many reasons for rashes, and many kinds of rashes.

Viruses are infectious microscopic agents that have a coating of RNA and DNA and so they can grow insides of the cells of humans and animals, which they certainly do, and this is why different anti-viral drugs are needed to fight them (as opposed to anti-bacterial drugs). They not only grow, but they can multiply and cause some awful diseases, and some of the diseases can end out being far worse than shingles. Some cause death. On its own, shingles doesn't usually cause death, but it can be a very slow recovery when a person has shingles. It's not the initial bout when the pustules are first seen that is, so much, the problem (though on one level, it is) because that part is temporary. It is the lengthy second part that stays around for months and months because of the neuralgia that is most remembered by anyone who has ever gone through shingles.

Fortunately, very few people have died because of shingles. The shingles can <u>contribute</u> to why a death occurs but the death will be for other reasons and the shingles would likely not be the sole cause. Shingles could tip the scales and cause death if something was already wrong, medically, with the person. Shingles is bad (i.e. it is an awful ordeal) but on its own, it is not so bad that it kills people . . . unless someone does not take care of him or herself when they have it. The person could die then, perhaps, but most people get medical care and then rest and will eat well enough when they get shingles and go through the ordeal.

Antibiotics use is tricky. There are hundreds of them and they come in different strengths or dosages. You have to take the right antibiotic for the right ailment. If you have an antibiotic laying around your home that was useful for a previous ailment, you do not use that antibiotic for a new and different ailment. Do not ever do that. It can be dangerous. Antibiotics are not made to be used that way—they are too diverse. They're all totally different and made for completely different ailments. The dosage often goes by the size and weight of the person, too. You do not ever want to take someone else's antibiotics, for that reason, and for other reasons as well. Get your own prescription, in other words. Also, it is true that many patients end out having a few left-over pills or capsules. This sometimes happens. Then, time goes by and after a time, which will vary with the different pills and capsules, the pills will be out of date. Effectiveness expires. The pills can lose their potency. You do not want to use those pills or capsules. You will need a new prescription.

If you come down with the same ailments the drug you still have had been used for or you have a different ailment, go see the doctor again. He will then diagnose the problem, and subsequently prescribe a <u>current</u> drug (or drugs because sometimes there are two or three prescriptions needed for a particular ailment). You should not use the pills or capsules that are old. Absolutely, do not use real old prescriptions. People do this rather frequently and it can get them into trouble.

It is usually not addicts who use old prescriptions. It is people who come down with a flare-up they may have had several months back or even years ago—like a prostrate or urinary problem or a gallstone or kidney-related issue. They may need quick help and relief because of the flare-up before they can even get in to see a doctor for a new prescription. They may be under great distress with painful symptoms. So, they'll use old pills. They want quick pain relief so they grab old medicine and/or medication. The problem with this scenario is that they could have a completely different condition, needing one or more different prescriptions. Everything needs to be properly diagnosed by a medical professional, particularly a physician, before your older pills are taken. You could be causing your body harm by taking older pills.

Taking such pills that are yours and are outdated and for the same condition is not against the law, per se, but it could be quite problematic and it is not a wise course. The wise course is to get to the doctor's office quickly and get diagnosed and get any new prescriptions. Capsules with powdered medicine or medication in them can deteriorate faster than compacted pills. In hot climates, both pills and capsules deteriorate faster than they do in colder climates but high humidity can really deteriorate pills faster. All pills and capsules have a shelf life.

At one time, certain prescriptions ended out allowing for a few extra pills/capsules but this is not done, so much, anymore because doctors know how many pills/capsules to prescribe for their patients now, and there are fewer and often, no grace pills are allowed. Still, sometimes people will not use up all the pills or capsules and so there may be a few left over. Some people are pill or capsule-shy and only take as many pills or capsules as they think are needed. Then, they end out with left-over ones. Also, if a second renewal prescription is needed, it may include more pills than are necessary and so those pills will be left over.

To clarify, there is a difference between a pill and a capsule. A pill is a compressed hardened mass having different sizes and shapes. Often, they are small and round. Some pills have a rounded oblong shape to them. Some oblong-shaped pills can be really large. I call them horse pills. The Valacyclover® pills I took, which seemed to cause the virus to rein back in and return to my backbone area, were large but they weren't the size of horse pills. They were capsule pills, which encapsulate and protect a powdered drug content. Capsules tend to be a rounded oblong shape. They have a hardened outer plastic-ish shell with powdered drugs inside them. I use the word, plastic-ish because the plastic ends out breaking apart in the stomach and so it is soluble and absorbs with the stomach's content.

For patients, they should not play Russian roulette with pill or capsule taking. The field of prescriptions is mumbo-jumbo to anyone who hasn't done adequate study of the subject and hasn't learned more about the subject than they think they know. Physicians are the knowledgeable ones. Doctors studied drugs in medical school plus they have their residency program, which is always under the supervision of other doctors. Doctors have to pass board exams, too. Most doctors go into practice right away so they don't forget what they have been learning. They do not get rusty. By practice, I don't, necessarily, mean private practice. They could go to work in a clinic or a hospital. All the different types of antibiotics and anti-viral meds have to be studied, and then there are all the painkillers, which again, are totally different from the medicines. To a large extent, after they start working as a physician, they will also learn as they go.

Painkillers are used to kill pain not germs or viruses (but some may inadvertently kill some germs, depending on the germs or even the viruses). When it comes to learning about drugs, there are different prescriptions for germs (bacteria) versus viruses, which also adds to the complication. You practically have to have a photographic memory to be able to remember and adeptly juggle all the different prescriptions. Doctors have medical books at their office, usually. They check up on medicine and medication rather often. They research whatever they have to. Doctors now have the benefit of the Internet (just like the patients do). If you think that doctors do not read some of what is on the Internet, think again. They do this rather often. Also, they usually have quite a few medical books at their own residence. Furthermore, doctors have other doctors to share information with. All doctors are right in the thick of things, which is a good place for them to be.

It seems like I should have had an actual low-dosage painkiller all along the way—i.e. an opioid in a milder form and with just enough strength to stop the bad pain when it would hit. I'm not the type to acquire an addiction (but, who is the type because addiction can happen to anyone). I keep wondering, though, can a painkiller, because of its chemical composition, reduce the effect of the anti-viral drug that is being used to curb the shingles virus and is that why a doctor might not give out that kind of a painkiller for shingles? I am sure doctors who are in research have well-studied these types of issues. For myself, I'm so opposed to that kind of thing (i.e. getting addicted to anything). I have drug-use phobia, and always have. I even wrote a book—*The Diary of a Drug Addict*—about drug rehabilitation and to help drug-addicted people. (I'm a trained counselor, educated in the field.)

As shingles are a short-term condition, opioid addiction doesn't stand too much of a chance of starting up. You would only need the pills for about a month. I'm a smidge upset with my doctor, who may be <u>too</u> leery about prescribing opioids for genuine painful conditions. But, should I be? His tendency to be so cautious is admirable, on the one hand, but on the other hand, if pain is present, why not prescribe a low-dosage painkiller? Is there something I don't know about? Or, could he have prescribed something more 'helpful' to buffer or rid me of the early-on pain? Many people around the U.S. are pondering questions that relate to their medical care and prescription drugs. Certainly, fewer opioids are being prescribed and this is distressing people who have real pain but do not get adequate pain relief. The doctor I have does seem good at assessing and prescribing but why did I end out suffering so much pain for at least a month?

Most people who want or request painkillers are not even close to being addicts. Some will even want to keep drugs at a distance, like I do. It is really the addicts that doctors should zone in on, not your average drug-fearing citizen. True, anyone can get addicted to a drug at any time but not usually for short-term use. Presently, even if painkillers and opioids get prescribed, the dosage could end out being lower than it would have been in the past. High-dose prescriptions are down by about an eighth (by twelve or thirteen percent), but overdose statistics are not down all that much—not proportionately. Of course, the lower-dosage prescriptions cost just as much as the other ones did. In truth, some people may need the higher-dose prescription but they are not receiving it from the doctor or medical professional. This is what has been happening, too often. Doctors have become skittish about prescribing medicine, most particularly, opioids.

Doctors can get fined if they prescribe in wrong ways, especially when it concerns opioids. My doctor just happens to be one of those ultra-cautious doctors who, I'm sure, wants to avoid fines at any cost because they can be imposed on doctors by monitoring medical and government agencies. Quite a few doctors are thusly inclined these days (i.e. they are ultra-cautious) because so many patients have died of opioid addiction and overdose. Some of this made the national News. I, at least, suspect that I could have been prescribed a moderate painkiller. Again, are doctors aware of something I am unaware of? Well, what can you do about it . . . but that is scary because many doctors have become too prescription leery, relative to opioids/painkillers.

Some doctors fear prescribing opioids, and certain other pills. Some people have to have these pills. People commit suicide if their physical pain gets to be too much and especially if it's chronic. Some patients should always have a pain medication. Doctors have a different outlook if they know pain is chronic. Any cancer patients, for example, if there are no reversals, will get pain medication on a regular basis. Thankfully, shingles are not a chronic condition. Any pain slowly and gradually subsides. The patient knows the neuralgia is going to go away and so does the doctor.

Also, doctors realize their patients can't do anything for themselves, if chronic pain is too acute. Everything around a patient's house gets behind. As a result, uncleanliness and poor hygiene and not eating well, or eating at all, can happen. When you have pain, movement is difficult. So is falling asleep. If you are on medication, including a painkiller, you may be extra tired, or lethargic. A painkiller can, perhaps, still enable you to do some tasks and possibly get what is essential done. Some people end out hiring someone to come in and help them, if they have pain that is hard to live with and that causes survival setbacks. Doctors are well aware of these situations. They make recommendations, relative to solutions to these related problems.

Many people come to depend on opioids because they have chronic pain, but they aren't necessarily, addicted to the painkiller(s)—not per se. They just <u>depend</u> on the medication (i.e. they need it to minimize, void out, and get rid of their pain). Dependency is not, necessarily, addiction, if you see the difference. Addiction is a medical issue. Dependency is more of a psychological matter. It may have little to do with choice, if there is chronic, awful pain.

When it comes to prescriptions, you have to just grin and bear it because you're under the doctor's care. In my case, changing doctors was a possibility, but I liked my doctor. Still, there is this other side of the coin and there is this rather obvious issue, which is that of the non-prescribing of stronger painkillers that might be truly needed. I had never had one problem with taking opioids or anything similar, either. Nothing is on my medical record to that affect—not even close. I'd had morphine for a complicated surgery I had close to fifteen years ago, but that was it. With the shingles, I really had little pain relief. Maybe doctors don't really know how much shingles hurt. If you haven't had them, you just can't know. I had them on both front and back. They hurt, doubly.

Well, now you know what shingles are—at least, generally. If you never got chickenpox and never had the chickenpox immunization, you could be all right, unless you get exposed to the chickenpox Varicella-zoster virus. If you had chickenpox and never had the chickenpox immunization, you are not safe from getting shingles. You can still get chickenpox again, or to shingles. You could get a chickenpox or a shingles immunization now. See what the doctor says. Find out where immunizations are given and go get whatever immunization the doctor suggests or is allowed. You'll have to fill out a form and a health-care professional will have to approve you for the immunization. Ask the health-care provider if you should get the chickenpox shot, or the shingles shot.

If you want to prevent shingles, if you are fifty years or older, a preventative shot will make it so that if you do get shingles, it will be in a very mild form and will not last long. You may not even have that happen, however. If you never had chickenpox, a preventative shot will help to keep you from getting chickenpox, and from getting shingles. One particular immunization is actually a chickenpox vaccine, not really a shingles vaccine, per se, but it will still hold shingles back or at bay because if you are not apt to get chickenpox, you are not apt to get shingles. The two vaccines are different, but they have some similarity, relative to their composition. They are not entirely similar, though. Again, talk to a physician about which immunization will be best for you. A physician has to know the patient's history.

People who had chickenpox will get the shingles vaccine to prevent them from getting shingles but they should talk to a health-care professional before they have the vaccine. People who never had chickenpox will want to get the chickenpox vaccine, early on, before they get chickenpox. If someone had chickenpox and never had the immunization, they will harbor the chickenpox virus and they should get the shingles immunization. The shingles shot is a <u>variation</u> of the chickenpox shot. Again, the two immunizations are not the same, so see a doctor about both.

If you had shingles (and you are likely older if you did), you will seek out the shingles shot, not the chickenpox shot. Again, explain your situation to the medical professional so you will get the right immunization. Get it all written down so you do not get confused. Even write down the name of the recommended immunization (i.e. Shingrix® or Zostervax®, aka Zostavax®). Check both out (and see Chapter 3). Whether the health-care professional recommends the chickenpox immunization, or the shingles shot, will relate to your medical history and your age. Shingles immunizations are generally for older people. You generally get the chickenpox immunization when you are younger. Again, the two shots have a similarity, but they are different. One is a little older than the other one is and only requires one immunization. Vaccines or immunizations can be given orally, or by shot. Both of the shingles vaccines are given, by shot. You may not need a shingles immunization if you had shingles because if you had a clear and obvious case of shingles, if you ever get it again, it will be a mild form of it anyway, because you already had it. Still, talk to the doctor about getting a bona fide shingles shot.

Some people who are older and who get shingles (which, again, is when people are apt to get them) could be vulnerable to cancer so they must keep their immune system tip-top while they have the shingles, and then, thereafter. <u>Getting shingles is a warning—that you'd better eat well, drink healthy liquids, get enough vitamins, avoid bad foods, sleep and rest enough, and avoid stress.</u>

The shingles, because a cellular battle was going on, likely added to my immune system problems (I got the shingles in the first place because my immune system was not up to par and I was going through a time of stress). Pain will also stress your immune system. When there's pain, the cells in your immune system are activated. The pain areas need help from cells. This can make you tired. Pain weakens you. The disease of shingles weakens you. When nerves get damaged (because of shingles), cell activity has to repair them. A battle is going on in your body and so you feel weaker, physically. You hope that any good bacteria that live inside your body will be able to fight off any bad bacteria, whenever your immune system is down. You have both types of bacteria and microbes in your body (i.e. good, and bad types). This is aside from any viruses you might have.

You have to eat vitamin smart when you have shingles but you might be too weak to fix a decent meal. Try to get to the grocery store. Get some of those nutritional beverages that come in a pack. Combo vegetable drinks are good (i.e. those fruits mixed with vegetables beverages). Regular vegetable juice is good to drink, too. Vegetable soup is good. Make sure fruit is around, especially citrus. Eat some oranges. Ant kind of avocado is good to eat, too. Some type them as a fruit, as some will also type tomatoes. Always, protein is important. Et al. and etc. Regularly eat well, day and night. Certain vitamins particularly help the immune system. Get some good vitamins into your body, one way or another. Keep to buying balanced food, and to balanced eating.

Vitamin D helps your immune system but as a person gets older, they will need more Vitamin D. You get Vitamin D from eating fatty fish (good fats), like salmon, mackerel, tuna, sardines (in the fish oil), egg yolks, beef liver, and from drinking milk. Older people will often reduce their Vitamin D intake, not increase it. They don't mean to. It just happens. Milk is a wonder beverage and always has been. With less or not enough Vitamin D, and an immune system that is weakened, an older person is more vulnerable to having a shingles flare-up, especially someone who hasn't increased their Vitamin D intake after they've started to age and have started to get in the elderly range. You don't want too much Vitamin D but you always have to have enough of it, for your age and size. Many will take a Vitamin D supplement but certain foods really have to be eaten and certain beverages have to be consumed.

Vitamin D also helps bones and muscles to strengthen, and older people need vitamins that help both since bone density reduces and muscles weaken, with age. Vitamin D is not in all that many foods. Some foods have it, but not very much of it so you have to eat what is higher in it. You have to have Vitamin

D in your body so you can absorb the Calcium that enters your body. There are actually three different forms of Vitamin D so you have to eat a variety of Vitamin D foods. The liver and the kidneys help with processing Vitamin D, which is one reason why the liver is so important. The sun's affects help a body to process Vitamin D. The sun helps a body to produce Vitamin D. Shut-ins, therefore, are more apt to get shingles because they rarely go outside.

Most people get enough Vitamin D if they eat a balanced diet. It is when a person gets into the senior citizen range that they will need to concentrate on increasing their intake of Vitamin D. Being consistent in eating key foods that have Vitamin D in them is extremely important, too. In other words, if you go six months with little Vitamin D (or even fewer months), you can be weakening or harming your body. Sunshine may not help all that much if there's little to no Vitamin D in your body. Certain fruit juices and health and nutrition bars are Vitamin D-fortified. Read all labels. Even read milk labels. Check out certain dark, leafy vegetables for Vitamin D amounts, too; some are high in Vitamin D.

Vitamin D can help to prevent certain diseases, one being shingles, but getting shingles can come about for other reasons, too. Vitamin D lack seems to be a very strong contributing factor, though. Other vitamin lacks can relate, as well. Not eating real well and eating a balanced diet could well be what brings shingles on. Older people, unfortunately, don't always eat as well as they should, for a number of reasons. They are weary more often and don't tend to their own eating all that diligently. Some older people aren't thusly inclined, but it can be a trend with a number of older people. Some older people stop cooking. Some of them don't go to the store as often as they once did. Some may lose a spouse so that many tasks do not get done like they once did.

Physicians have noted that there are three vitamins to especially take, preferably in combination, and these three would be Vitamin A, Vitamin C, and Vitamin E. (ACE is easy to remember.) This would include Beta-carotene because it will convert to Vitamin A, when it gets into the body. If you get shingles, depending on your size, you will need to get A, C, and E into your body on a regular basis because they are believed to help to relieve shingles pain and irritation. You have to learn how much of each vitamin you will need and work them into your diet. Anything that relieves pain in a natural way will be worth looking into. Again, take the three vitamins in combination and at the same time.

By now, you are aware that shingles stays painful for some time. It isn't that there is a sudden healing with them or that one morning you'll just wake up and feel like everything is fine. But the day will eventually come when you'll rub your hand over the skin area where all the pustules were and are now dried up and the nerve pain there will feel less intense. Still, it is a very slow mend. It just goes way slower than you will be expecting the healing to go. You have to be real patient. Maybe the nerves heal up more while you are sleeping and are at rest, assuming you are not moving around. I put a long pillow to one side of me so I would not be able to move or turn over in my sleep but I made sure the pillow did not put any pressure on my nerve-damaged areas. For the longest time, even slight pressure was painful.

Rest is important when you have shingles but you can't help but rest when you have them and when you're taking the neuralgia medicine. You're so tired. When you reach the point to where you experience just enough of a reduction of the nerve pain to be optimistic, you will be in better spirits. Malaise and lethargy will lift because it is the nerve pain that is causing most of the problems. This 'easier time of it' can range from three to six months after its onset, unless the particular case was not ever all that bad.

The reason why it was so hard for me to sleep was because even when I slept on the only unaffected side, on the left, gravity and the weight of my skin would push and pull the nerve-damaged areas in the other three areas and that weight pressure caused me pain. If I ever accidentally moved in my sleep and the nerve pain areas were jeopardized and especially if I rolled on top of where any of them were, the area would, thereafter, be very painful. Of course I would wake up. No pressure, at all, could be put on those three areas, even when I was sitting. I always had to lean forward when I worked at my desk, or when I sat in my upholstered chair. Shingles become <u>such</u> an inconvenience. And the pain areas were constantly distracting so I couldn't get away from what was constantly bothering me. Those three pain areas were where pressure or weight affected the damaged nerves. It was damaged nerves plus the weight and pressure that made sleeping difficult. When lying down, and from the gravity pull or the pressing and the pulling down of the skin, in areas, it was really hard to get comfortable. I could never really get all that comfortable.

There was nothing I could do about these three acute pain spots—absolutely nothing. I know other people have suffered worse, though, especially burn victims. I had to lie down from time to time and so the pain would just automatically be there. There were times when the shingles, literally, tormented me. There were times when I dreaded even having to go to bed. There were times when I was quite sure I needed a prescribed painkiller, hands down, but I did not have any around. The fact that shingles is an actual virus adds in, too, because again, an active virus makes a person ill, and I was ill and feeling poorly for quite some time. I had no one at home to help me but I pretty much would have had to have weathered the storm on my own, anyway. I am not exaggerating what I went through, either. It may seem like I have, to some people, but I have not. Those two areas where the pustules had been really did a number on me.

When the painful areas would be present even when I slept on the one good side, skin pressure on the nerves especially pressed against the backbone and agitated the nerves there, and it pressed against all the nerve-affected areas in front. There were nerve-pressed areas there, because of the gravity pull. Also, when I sat or stood, there would be heavier weighing and pressure on the whole area under my right breast (where one patch of shingles and nerve damage was) and the pressure from the right breast weighed down on those nerves and agitated them (for a long, long time). No matter what I did, I could not escape nerve-weight agitation on or alongside of certain areas—like, around the back area, along the area under the right breast, and wherever else skin weight would put pressure or where the pustules were (or had been, because they dried up, somewhat early on). The nerve damage where they had been stayed around, for some time.

These pressure spots got to where they would occasionally become acute pain and they would drive me up a wall. That is when I would get most upset because I didn't have any quick opioid-type painkiller on hand to quickly take. I needed something stronger than what I had because when I'd move or get in a different position, I would feel pain in those spots/areas. Many times, I had to move so slowly. I didn't need anything really strong, just something stronger than what I had on hand. After a time, if I stayed in one place, the pain would subside, but not if I was lying down. Loose skin and gravity pulled and pressed on the damaged and agitated nerves. Sleep got to be sporadic for me, and this ended out controlling my life and my schedule for a number of months. I didn't sleep for long periods of time, and my sleep was not always real deep sleep, either, and everyone needs that deep-sleep phase because it is so restorative. I woke up, too often.

People who work a 9 to 5 job had sure better have some co-workers and any managers around who are understanding if they get shingles (especially in certain places on the body). When anyone sits at a desk or table, they have to lean forward if shingles are anywhere on the back or even to the side. Workers may feel extra tired. They may need to be given less hours, for a time, or to leave early to go home and rest more. Initially, they may have to be out from work for a week or even two weeks. Of course, other ailments besides shingles can have this effect on people. When energy gets sapped, as happens with shingles, motivation can get sapped. It isn't something that a worker wants to happen. It just happens. Probably certain medicines and medications will do that, too, regardless of what they are for. But again, the virus itself will cause some fatigue so there is a double fatigue whammy—the prescription meds, and the virus.

Some types of work can be very dangerous if someone has shingles, especially physical-related work. Working can quickly add to fatigue. And then there is some discouragement along the way, too, and that doesn't help one bit. It can add some to any fatigue. All of this will eventually pass and if you're going through it, you keep wondering when the bulk of it will be over with. Anyone who has shingles has to keep in mind that, eventually, all will pass. It's just that the nerves take such a long time to heal.

I stayed inside the whole time I had the pustules. I was fortunate that I could. A few weeks into this shingles ordeal, however, and I just wanted to get outside, in the sun. I'd been holed up inside for so long . . . and my bedroom is very dark, which is the way I like it but I don't like being in a dark room for too very long. I wanted to be around bright colors and even just any colors. I wanted to get away from the gloom. The rest of my home is light enough but I had to rest and sleep more than usual during the shingles ordeal so I was in that dark bedroom for longer than I liked to be and really should have been. We all need light. Light and movement stirs up endorphins.

I hadn't been moving around much, at all, so not too many endorphins got charged up. Again, you can't lift or bend much, and you especially can't twist when you have front and back shingles. Walking is OK, up to a point. I'd been wanting to take an R and R break eventually, from all my work, but this wasn't quite what I'd had in mind and frankly, too much time got lost, relative to my work, and this bothered me, a lot. Still, life had to go on. There are times in life when you can't even have the piece of cake, let alone, the icing.

I had a temperature the whole time that I had the pustules, but it wasn't too high. It added to my weariness. And, I believe I had a temperature even after the pustules had dried up. I think that when the nerves are inflamed and there is pain, you are apt to have a raised temperature. You're going to be somewhat flushed. When nerves are inflamed and you are more tired because of that, you will be in bed more hours of the day than usual because you are more tired, and when you are in bed, the chances are greater that the nerve endings will get even more inflamed because of gravity pulling down on the skin.

Any amount of pain makes you slow down. Living becomes a strain. Pain hurts. No one likes it. You get despondent because you are powerless to make the pain go away and because the pain is constantly in your face. But, you press on, despite more weariness than usual and despite any accompanying malaise. Then, too, I was additionally tired because of my part-time sleeping. It was hard to even relax enough to fall asleep. I had to constantly re-maneuver myself to get into a better sleep position—on the one side only—and sometimes, there was no better position. Turning to the side an inch was about all I could do. Shingles can totally inconvenience you. And, if the nerve pain stays around for a long time, as mine did, the inconveniences become an everyday and prolonged issue. Shingles can be a nuisance, but so much will depend on the severity of the case. Mine just happened to show up in places that were extremely inconveniencing—on front <u>and</u> back.

Gravity would pull down on my skin in a number of ways and there would be some pain while sleeping, sitting, and standing, but while standing even more so because I would usually be moving when I stood. I had to be careful how I moved. I moved about very slowly. I moved around differently. Bouncing around was out of the question. At first, I took the Tylenol® 500 for pain relief and at times, it seemed to help, but only a little. I'd only bought the 24-capsules container and wish I'd bought the larger size one because I ended out using some of my ibuprofen 200 tablets because I'd had those from before. I took these ones two at a time. They totaled under 500, at 400 milligrams.

I so hoped the shingles would just suddenly stop being painful and distracting. A few spots where all the shingles pustules had been seemed more painful than other of the spots so I wondered if nerves under those spots might be more damaged. I did not know. They simply seemed to be more vulnerable to pulling and being pressed down on by the weight of my skin, as I moved about. Still, I kept hoping that the pain would all just suddenly go away and all the nerve damage would be repaired at the same time (by whatever in the body happens to do the repair). Would they even, ever, be repaired, I wondered, and would those areas ever cease to be so sensitive and painful to the touch?

Again, I'd read in one place that it could take several months for the neuralgia to go away. I'd read in one place that it could take up to a year before everything healed up, which caused me to have a quiet internal panic that I didn't share with anybody because I kept thinking that the neuralgia could possibly heal up sooner than that. (But it didn't.) The neuralgia subsided really slowly and it just kept staying around. Whereas rashes heal up really fast and there is no neuralgia from rashes, this is not the case with shingles. I had, at one time, believed the shingles would heal up, similarly to a rash, but the two conditions are not even close to being the same.

PART 3

Shingles stages, attempted remedies, and immunization

There are really three apparent stages of shingles. The first one is the initial flare-up of the virus and its attaching to the nerves and causing the pustules or blisters. That's when you must take the anti-viral medicine, usually in pill form. Again, I took the Tylenol® 500 at this time, as well, but a prescribed painkiller would have sure been nice. The second stage is when the blisters or pustules have dried up and the liquid went back into the skin. (You never touch the pustules. You never try to remove them.)

The third stage is the longest stage. It is when pain stays around, in places, and when it seems more obvious because some nerves have been compromised and irritated and even damaged. You really feel the nerve pain, especially because you have to get into certain positions all the time (because of resting, sleeping, sitting, standing, and moving about). Because of the collective pressure on the areas where the shingles are on the body and because of the skin shifting and the weight pressure, nerves get pressed and pulled and even pinched, at times, and so the pain becomes more acute in those places and it stands out and is constantly distracting. Most likely, the nerves are inflamed. You wonder if permanent damage is being done in those affected areas but you have no choice but to move around and lay down so it all just happens. All three stages are painful and difficult. During Stage 3, the pain slowly, at less than turtle pace, subsides, but it takes months, and then more months.

During any of the stages, people have been known to cry. I've heard that other people have cried, and I know I cried, mainly because it hurt so much when I was lying down and trying to move. I don't like to admit that I cried, but I did. I heard of one good-sized man who cried when he had shingles and I heard that from a woman who was living in the same home with the man, and not from the man. Men might not like to admit that they cried, because of shingles nerve pain.

I could have used an opioid prescription during Stage 3. Painkillers would have helped me sleep. I was never given a prescription for sleeping, but I never thought to ask for one. Acute pain is chronic during Stage 3 and there can sometimes be shooting or throbbing pain during Stage 3. The more often you accidentally sleep on a shingles area, the more pain there will be. It can build up. You can worsen the pain in an area if you accidentally lay down on that area. Any healing of it will go in reverse and it will, then, take even longer for the neuralgia to subside. Stage 2 extends into Stage 3 because you still have whole areas of neuralgia or nerve pain all around where the pustules/blisters had been before they dried up and went away. When pressure goes on those areas, it hurts a lot, but of course you try not to put pressure on those areas. Again, the actual affected area covers more area than it looks like it covers. Nerve attacks/damage goes out, some, from where the pustules are. I couldn't guess why. You'd think it would be the opposite and that it would be in, a little, instead.

In order to write this book, I have had to be a bit of a complainiac so I could get all the details in. (Not that there wasn't a lot to complain about.) I like to expose this and that but I don't really like complaining. Sometimes you have to complain, though. Sometimes plain writing (or talk) can be interpreted as complaining, when all that is really being done is educating or exposing or simply relaying and communicating.

Since I got shingles in front, back, and the pain extended to the one side, I was considerably handicapped. When they are on certain areas of the body, they are not so inconveniencing because little to no pressure is ever put on some and certain areas. I was much less able to move around than some other shingles-afflicted people may have been. The areas where pressure had been put (that became all the more damaged and painful as time went by), ended out being much slower to heal because of the constant pressing down on them, which had to be done, if I wanted to sleep. My shingles ended out taking such a long time to heal but it was technically the nerve damage that took such a long time to heal, which was well after the pustules had dried up and faded from my skin. As it turned out, even a year later, I could still feel nerve-area discomfort in both front and back but especially over my front ribs. It was only a little distracting, though, not like it had been earlier on (but it was still noticeable).

Years later, the areas on the front and back were still a little sensitive so I assume there had been some long-term damage but it is slight. I believe the slight sensitivity is always going to be there, or it would be gone by now (i.e. several years later as I am revising this book). I am able to live with it but it makes me feel a little beat up on (like other of my medical issues make me feel beat up on). When you age and get to a certain age, you feel beat up on—in body and mind. Living has a way of taking a toll on a person, over the years. They get 'beat up' with the passage of time. By a certain age, you are literally worn down, even if you appear fit. Sadly, aging does that to everyone.

One thing about the areas where the nerve pain was, you couldn't just suddenly scratch those areas without thinking because if you did, there would be burning pain. You would stop scratching pretty fast. With shingles, your skin will be itchy on occasion, as skin sometimes is. Out of habit, you'll scratch the area and the scratching will greatly aggravate the damaged nerves. You'll scratch without thinking. After doing that a few times, you won't do it again. You'll rub the itchy area really lightly, instead, hoping the itching will be relieved, and it usually is. You acquire a totally different way of scratching itches. The itching is sometimes because of the shingles but it may just be because of dry skin. However, with me, after quite a few months went by, the areas where the damaged nerves were started to itch on their own and not because of tiny microbes or bacteria being on my skin. The damaged nerves that were under my skin itched on their own and rather often, and this became quite disconcerting. It was manageable, but was very distressing.

Stage 1 is hard because you have a temperature and those unsightly pustules, which range in size. You worry that they will break open but again, as far as I know, mine never did. The pustules had a fairly thick exterior, or so it seemed. They dried up and blood had somehow been underneath. Seeing the big, dark scabs was a bit scary, I must admit. (I assume it was dried blood—unless the liquid that was in the pustules changed color somewhere along the way, which doesn't seem possible so it was likely dried blood.) I do not know what happened to the liquid. It seemed to have dried up and to have just gone back into my body. I earnestly do not believe any of the pustules burst on their own, even with the weight of my clothes but I never wore very heavy clothes because of the pressure that heavy clothes would have put on the irritating nerve areas. I'd actually feel some aggravation on the areas if I wore anything heavy, like a sweater. I'm glad I didn't get shingles in the winter. Mine occurred in the spring (so no heavy clothes were needed). I don't think that shingles tend to occur during any particular season, but perhaps weather is a factor. Again, it likely has more to do with a weakened and distressed immune system.

Something goes on with your immune system when you have pain past a certain point. You don't know it is happening. You can't see it happening. But your immune system is fighting and gets out of its usual equilibrium because of what it is fighting, and also because of any pain. Your immune system does not like pain. With shingles, the immune system is fighting because of the virus, and likely because of the nerve damage the virus leaves (that gets better with time). The immune system wants the virus inactivated and the nerves to be restored. That is its job. The immune system is a force inside your body. This force is on your side. It will manage the virus and will try to restore every nerve that has been damaged. Some of the nerves may get repaired faster than others do.

Whenever the immune system is more actively trying to help the body to be repaired, the affected person will get more tired than usual. Rest will continue to be important so anyone who ever gets shingles has to plan on having lots of rest. Even though more rest is forced on them, because they will be tired more often, people have to sometimes force themselves to rest so they can get better, faster. Our immune system is something we have to try to take care of. Rest is one way to do that.

In that your immune system had to have been weak right before you even got the shingles, your immune system is taking a double whammy and becomes even weaker because of the pain and the accompanying fatigue. You are not in a real good position. <u>You have to focus in on strengthening your immune system. It has to become a goal so you have to eat enough of certain foods—i.e. the ones that strengthen the immune system.</u> Spinach always helps. I'm big on spinach. Look in to some new foods—ones that especially help the immune system.

Several months into it, for the first time, I turned over to my bad side in my sleep. I thought it would be okay to do that because a part of that side seemed to have healed up some . . . but I was wrong. None of the nerves had healed up enough and this is the point. I was sleeping on that affected side for at least a few hours, I think, and my body weight bore heavy down on those damaged nerves and gravity pulled down on my skin. When I woke up, not only was that side really painful but the areas in front and back next to and near that side area were extra painful, too, and I was in agony that whole day and for a time, thereafter. Live and learn. Don't do too much too soon.

Until the nerves are completely healed, you cannot sleep on top of a compromised neuralgia site. It's tempting to do that when you think things might be better, but do not do that because the nerves are still damaged and you can increase the damage if you put any pressure, at all, on any neuralgia site. You cannot sit back on a chair, even if it is upholstered. <u>Maybe</u> a soft down pillow could be placed there and you could sit back on the chair, then, but I'm not even that sure about that. I just always sat upright and leaned over when I was in a chair, which is what I do when I work at my desk, anyway, because I write so much.

Any agitation setback like what I experienced after sleeping on the side that had some, but not enough improvement, slowed down the nerve-damage healing (because it had increased the damage). Thereafter, I continued to sleep only on the one safe side, no matter what. This got to be boring and exasperating. Even if areas that had had the pustules or blisters on them started to <u>seem</u> better, they were still very vulnerable areas. That nerve damage and irritation is like nothing I'd ever experienced. It's not good to get impatient, but you do, and it does little good. Keep the pressure off of any affected areas, all the time. It's hard to not turn in your sleep. This is the problem. We are all used to doing that. Even if you prop a pillow to one side, you can still turn and agitate the affected nerves (adding more to the pain).

For sure do not accidentally bump into anything so the area where the nerve pain is gets bumped. Bumping is bad. I was lucky—that did not happen to me. I accidentally did that when I had surgery but not when I had shingles. I was extra careful. As a strict reminder, you absolutely do not want more inflammation than there already is or the healing will take even more time. You want the nerve damage to heal up as fast as possible so you can start to allow pressure on those affected areas, and rest and sleep better. You want no residual pain to be present in the affected areas but that might happen anyway because, again, when you sleep, the weight of your skin goes downward and so, some nerve-damage areas can get that weight pressure and pull and consequently, the neuralgia will be slower to heal and will continue to cause some pain and aggravation. (This pressure and pulling happened to me after I'd had surgery, too—call it the Weight Pressure Pain Principle.) I have written a book about the surgery I had (titled *The Surgery Experience*). With that book, the weight pressure pain was principally because of a large cut that had gone through my skin and because of the rib splitting and the moving and pushing back of a muscle during the surgery (and the possible cutting of it and stitching it back up) and the pain likely had nothing to do with damaged nerves in so far as I know. But nerves where there was any cutting had to have been damaged around those incised areas.

As with the surgery book, I ended out doing this write-up over a period of time and so there ended out being some repetition because I sometimes forgot what I wrote, but any repetition tends to be in a different context anyway so it is generally all right. Not feeling well and being in pain while writing about both my surgery and my shingles was a bit difficult because in both cases, my concentrative focus was not as good as it could have been. I thought to myself, 'well, I'll just fix everything later in the write-ups (books)', which I tried to do. About six months after the shingles flared up, the often distracting nerve pain was a little less painful but still, it was generally pronounced, but then, if I rolled over and slept on any of the bad spots, I would be back to square one, reference the stressful pain. It can be hard, writing a book, when you have shingles. I had to rest a lot, so I forgot what I previously wrote but, I reasoned, 'the show (or the writing) must go on'. I was writing a number of other books, too, at the same time.

My shingles experience had similarities to my surgery experience, I soon realized. Pain was no fun, in both cases, and healing came very slow, in both cases. Pain was managed as well as possible during my surgery, which was twelve or so years before I got the shingles and that makes a difference because there was no opioid crisis, then. I am one to discontinue painkiller use as soon as possible because I secretly don't like to take any drugs at all and I have always felt that way. I worry about side effects, too. You want to take as low a dosage as possible for any ailment. That is my belief . . . but, you also want what you need, if pain is real bad. If you have pain that is a 7 out of 10, you don't want a pain-reliever that only helps with a 2 or 3 pain. I never used to think neuralgia was that painful. Often, it isn't and it only concerns a small area and is of a slight pain magnitude, but the neuralgia I had in those two areas, with shingles, was different.

As I think more deeply about the neuralgia, it seems that any pressure put on the nerve site (or sites) was either further damaging the nerves or it was agitating the already-damaged nerves and not really damaging them more. Either way, it was not good. If you accidentally roll on a shingles area during sleep, when you wake up, it feels like they are considerably more damaged because it hurts, horribly. If you ever get the front and back shingles, again, even when you sleep on the safe side, areas will still hurt because of skin weight pulling and pressing that is affecting them, in places.

Because the healing of the neuralgia goes so slowly, you truly start to wonder—am I going to always be debilitated by this nerve damage? Could I even end out being partly handicapped? At one point, I started to feel like that because one night, I accidentally rolled over to one of the bad areas, again, while I was sleeping. I'd forgotten to put the large pillow in place. Quite a few nerves seemed way more agitated in more places afterwards and it was all very distressing. I truly needed painkillers then, but there were none and I was suffering and thinking about changing doctors. But I didn't. I hadn't gone in to see him about the pain in an effort to get more adequate pain relief because I didn't think I could. I believed I would be declined. Maybe I should have put up a fuss.

Nobody wants to feel pain all day long, and then, again, during the night. This whole shingles ordeal is truly like being handicapped, physically. Your life has to totally center on the shingles. Again, your sleep is constantly interrupted and you only sleep three or four hours at a time when you get the shingles on the front and back, and they extend over to the side. Because the pain caused me constant distraction and malaise, I ended out working less efficiently and I realized that this was psychologically hard on me. My writing helped me to not be as distracted as I could have been. It helped the time go by faster. In a sitting position, I could write for hours . . . until I felt sleepy. Writing helped me to block out my pain. I don't know what I would have done, had I not have been able to sit so much.

People who have shingles in different areas may have a totally different experience from the one I had. So much depends on where the shingles show up. Some people who had shingles may not be able to relate to my experiences all that well, or they may be able to relate only in part. Much will depend on the medicine and medication they go on, too. Also, some shingles patches are fairly small. When you hear that someone has or has had shingles, realize that every shingles case is different and can range from the more simple case to the more complex case (or the less painful case to the more painful case). My problem was with sleeping, and with the pressing and pulling on the sites so the neuralgia was constantly being compromised.

Right or wrong, I felt I <u>needed</u> a moderate painkiller. I assume my doctor did not think I was in that much pain, or that I was going to be in that much pain when he prescribed what he did, which was very weak in the painkilling department. I wanted something more pain-relieving but, again, I did not end out getting any opioid painkillers. You really can't twist a doctor's arm but maybe I should have taken more time to articulate what I was going through? But, there's sometimes pressure there because doctors are in and out of side rooms, fast, when they are booked with patients. What you say you must sometimes say quickly.

Also realize that doctors are always concerned that a non-addicted patient could become addicted and they do not want to be responsible for that happening. This has happened to many a physician. Some doctors had their arms twisted, by patients. Some patients ended out dying from an overdose because of genuine over-prescribing. Some doctors ended out going to prison so you can understand why doctors are concerned and will air on the side of caution. Still, when there's pain, there's pain.

I had pain because of my wearing a bra, too. For women (depending on where the shingles are), wearing a bra can be very difficult, if not impossible. A part of my front shingles were up against the bra-line so I had to ride the bra up a half inch or a little more so the bra wouldn't press on that shingles spot, but the bra pulled on the shingles area and that constantly agitated the nerves there. I put my back bra strap way up high on my back, too, so it would not touch the shingles on the back, but it pulled somewhat on them, anyway. On the side area, I pushed the side of the bra up as high as it would go so it would not be on top of where the nerve pain was. For the front-area problem, I had to make the straps go as tight as they would go so there would be less weight coming down on the shingles site that was over the ribs and under my right breast. In other words, I <u>had</u> to wear a bra so the right breast would be pulled up and not fall flat down on that front shingles site and cause even more nerve pain and damage because of the weight, and I had to constantly keep positioning the bra so it would not rub against the nerve-damage sites in front, to the side, and the back.

Wearing a bra became just another constant aggravation. I had to wear a bra all the time so the front-area neuralgia would be less affected by pressing-down weight. I had to wear the bra a certain way—not the usual way a bra is worn. Women that have a medical problem (like shingles, or a surgery) that results in a bra-wearing situation, have to wear good bras that adjust well and fit well and comfortably. This was a problem for me when I had my surgery, too, because I was cut open at the side and my ribs were split so surgical work could be done from that angle.

If you didn't wear a bra and you were a woman with shingles, there would be more pressure on the nerves from the skin weight but if you wore it, you'd have to totally adjust it in places on your body and there would still be some pressure points, mostly in front. Because of the bra adjustments, it was not comfortable wearing the bra (but again, I had to wear the bra). I would still end out with some pain, even with an adjusted bra that was regularly moved-around to avoid any pain areas. Men do not have to contend with this problem. Bras give women a better posture so women do not like not being able to wear them, especially if they wear a larger cup-size bra. I went to a different bra style than I usually wear so there would be less nerve agitation. This is what I had to do when I'd had my surgery, too, because of where the incision was and where the pain areas were. My incision had been at the side, where my ribs got split. Changing bra styles made some difference but wearing a bra was still problematic.

Wearing a bra can easily add some extra nerve inflammation. It's a Catch-22 situation. Again, I pushed mine very high up on the sides and back when I wore a bra so the neuralgia areas would not be further harmed by the back and side strap. Again, I tightened the top straps so the front part of the bra would move up more and be less compromising of that front area under my right breast.

You might want to remove the wire on the bra on the side where the shingles are, if there is a wire in your bra and you have neuralgia around there. These wires used to be metal, but now they are plastic. You can put it back in later.

Stage 3 shingles can be as or almost as painful as Stage 1 and Stage 2. You'll have damaged nerve endings that continually send pain messages to your brain. The continued nerve pain is known as post-therpetic neuralgia. From the onset of shingles, the worst part of it can last (on average) from three weeks to three months. This is what I experienced, but the main ordeal can last as long as six months. With me, I still had the neuralgia a year later, but it wasn't painful by that time. One spot was, a little—right under my right breast, which was no surprise. That area had constantly been agitated, even with my best efforts. Still, by that time, the worst part of the ordeal was, essentially, over with.

Once most of or all of the nerve pain goes away, you can go in and get an anti-shingle virus immunization to prevent them from recurring or from recurring very badly. You have to wait until your shingles bout is completely over with (though there may still be slight nerve damage). As previously noted, there are at least two types of shots out there for people. Learn which one you need from your doctor. If you've had chickenpox, you can get a shot before you come down with shingles, which is <u>highly</u> advisable.

There are two post-shingles immunizations that will hold back another bout of shingles. Zostervax®, aka Zostavax®, is for people over 60; Shingrix® is for people over 50. This seems strange to me because some people who are 50 seem 60 and some people who are 60 seem 50. (I think medical condition and strength of someone's immune system could factor in.) Still, there is this option for some and one of them could have better effect. The first-noted immunization is a living vaccine (live viruses); the second one is a non-living one (dead viruses). You'll need to research both (and talk to a doctor). Both last for up to five years but you can still get a case of shingles; it just won't be too bad of a case. Your chances of not getting shingles, at all, are considerably decreased.

It's best to talk with your Primary-Care physician about <u>both</u> types of shots and to discuss any possible risks and side effects with the doctor. (You must always do this in advance, with any immunization.) They may only have one of them at the place where you go but you'll still want to learn about both. <u>Had I known what I was going to go through, I would have gone in and been vaccinated earlier (like in my twenties or thirties and certainly, by my fifties).</u> Shingrix® just came in for use in 2017 but Zostervax® came in, in 2006. It worked for a half of the people who got the shot. Shingrix® came out soon after and gave over ninety-five percent prevention for the first year and around eighty-five percent prevention for the next five years. With Shingrix®, two doses are needed, six months apart. Insurance will cover these shots (unless someone's immune system is poor, but even if it is, some insurance might still pay for it. A nationalized medicine program is apt to pay for it . . . but check, first. Who knows what the future holds, reference preventative efforts? Everyone hopes for something that will kill the virus and eradicate it (like the smallpox vaccine did with smallpox).

As previously noted, there is an actual chickenpox immunization given to younger people and children. In fact, the first immunization can be given at age one. It is obviously quite different than the two shingles types that are ordinarily for older people and that are manufactured especially for shingles. The one for young people and children is anti-chickenpox.

Chickenpox is highly contagious—not only from the liquid in the pustules or blisters, but even from just breathing. No parent should allow themselves to be immunization-shy for their child. Some parents are and they shouldn't be unless a particular one is especially iffy and questionable. Make sure your children are up to date on all essential immunizations but research all of them, first, just to be safe. The chickenpox immunization may have to be given separate from the school, however. Make sure your child gets this immunization when they are very young, <u>before</u> they come down with chickenpox.

Measles is another very important immunization for children to have. Measles is dangerous and can cause some serious medical problems. They have a series of measles immunizations. For sure, two are needed two different times. A third may be needed. Some types can differ, relative to administration. Check with a doctor. Measles shots have to be timely, as with any chickenpox immunization. Children are exposed to these germs when they are around other school children. Odds are higher, in other words, that they will be exposed.

Soon after they started giving COVID shots to children, a number of children began to get upper-respiratory problems and a strange new illness started up. It caused breathing problems and had other symptoms, as well. They gave children COVID shots after adults had been given vaccinations and after that, they started giving them to babies (though they were not required). Health officials considered the vaccinations to be safe for those younger and dosage amount was adapted to the age and weight. This is done with other vaccinations, too. Always age and weight is considered but there is usually a range (amount) relating to those younger and those older. Obviously a shot for a baby is going to be very different than a shot for an adult. Concerning the shingles shot, parents should try to get their child(ren) in before they are exposed to the chickenpox virus and when they are old enough to have it. The race is on to get them in to have that vaccination because who knows when they might be exposed to the related virus? Who knows when they would be exposed to any virus? If they are in school, their chances increase significantly.

Different countries still get bouts of measles cases from time to time. Measles crop up in the U.S. from time to time. They can be confused with chickenpox. Measles spread fast. So does chickenpox. Find immunization clinics around where you live if certain ones aren't given at school by the school nurse or a visiting doctor. Talk with the school nurse to learn about immunizations and their short-term and long-term scheduling. Don't put either immunization off. Once upon a time, all school immunizations were free, and they were always put on a shot record for the kids and parents. They used to give out a hand-sized folder to the pupils to give to their parents. It had all the shots on record and verified. It was yellow. It was never good to lose these. They need to always be in a safe place that is easy to get to. Shot records should always be handy. Never throw them away.

You can get a measles immunization when you are an older child, and when you are an adult, and you should. If you get measles as an adult, you can end out with encephalitis (inflammation of the brain), and also with pneumonia. Before the immunization for measles, millions of people around the world died because of measles, every year. Measles is communicable. You can get it even after someone who has measles has left a room because of aerial germs. When a disease affects respiration, pneumonia can set in. A high temperature will factor in. It is never good to get fluid in either lung. That is a very bad sign. This can happen if pneumonia sets in. It doesn't always happen, but it can. This can even happen when someone gets the flu.

With the coronavirus (COVID), the virus attacks the lungs and causes inside fluid leak in the lungs so the liquid retards the breathing. Fluid gets into air sacs; it leaks from blood vessels that are in the lungs. Increasing sepsis can, then, occur. Poor breathing, of course, affects the heart. How much liquid can leak from blood vessels in the lungs? What can be done about this liquid? Can liquid come in to the lungs in any other way? If the effects of COVID-19 and its variants and sub-variants goes past a certain point, these complications can set in. The body fighting the virus is a separate issue from this lung fluid problem. The lung fluid problem creates a need for a ventilator or respirator. How exactly that fluid gets into the air sacs to begin with is <u>the</u> key question. Only certain doctors would be able to explain that. Also, how and when does the fluid in the lungs form? Exactly where does the fluid form? Why does fluid leak from blood vessels in the lungs? How can sepsis be stopped? These are key questions, and there are key questions relating to shingles, too, but the shingles virus is generally under control.

When it comes to medical matters, finding information on key questions, and getting actual specifics, can be like finding a needle in a haystack, even on the Internet. Much on the Internet is general and surface and for lay people.

You have to dig. You have to think. There are medical libraries at medical schools, which can be helpful.

Fluid in a lung is hard to get rid of and sometimes, if it seems gone, it can return. It may be hard to detect it, depending on the situation. If it returns, you get back to the hospital, fast. The coronavirus is one that brings about pneumonia and fluid in a lung (or in both lungs). We are all very aware, now, of viral respiratory diseases, particularly because of the coronavirus (COVID-19 and its variants/sub-variants). We know all about respirators and ventilators now, too. Again, shingles is not a respiratory disease. It relates to nerves, and the skin (Neurology, and Dermatology).

Again, you get what I call post-therpetic neuralgia during Stage 3 of Shingles but you have neuralgia during Stages 1 and 2, as well. I wasn't upset about the neuralgia and pain so much until Stage 3 and after the blisters and pustules had disappeared. As noted before, I do not recall any of the pustules breaking open. I had assumed the nerve pain would go away after the pustules were gone (but the pain didn't leave). (I was sure glad to see the pustule areas go because they were so dark.) Stage 3 is when you, pretty much, stop or slow down in your taking any pain medication (if you have any and it may only be aspirin that you've taken).

Again, the nerves in some areas get pressed down on or pinched some by skin weight bearing down on them or pulling at them, especially when the person is resting or sleeping. Anyone with shingles has to be expecting this to happen, despite the severity of the case. Wherever they are pressed down on or pulled and meet with resistance, those areas will end out being the more painful areas. These pains are different from the primary neuralgia-related pain. They are added pains (and pain on top of the neuralgia pain). For me, these pains were along edges, like the backbone or any area where my skin weighed down on as I was lying down or even sitting. They can be under the bra area with women who get shingles in front because the pressure and weight from the breast naturally presses down on the nerve-damaged area that is in the front area, higher up. Again, that one area will always take longer to heal

63

because the nerve damage doesn't get as much of a chance to get repaired. It keeps getting rubbed against or pressed down on by a breast.

Certain areas just keep getting agitated by the skin weighing down, and by gravity. Repeated agitation can make healing near-impossible when it comes to any nerve damage. At some point in time, affected people will wonder if the nerve damage is going to be permanent. I know I did, after a month or two, because the nerve healing was going so slow.

I tried wearing a snug whole slip that I happened to have (and no bra) and the slip held some of the skin more in place so there was less of a chance for there to be pressure pain, but there still was some pain; it was just a little less. Men could wear a slightly snug undershirt, but it can't be tight because the nerve-damaged areas can become inflamed and anyone who has shingles will want to avoid that during all of the three stages. Men who have extra weight on them will have a problem with the skin weighing down on nerve-damaged areas. Even if there is little extra weight, this will happen. It will happen to any person. Skin weighing down will add some pain. It stresses the damaged nerves.

After three months of having the nerve-ending pain, I was truly wondering if it would ever be gone. I'd wondered this earlier, but why was the pain still present (in both back and front)? I was getting so tired of living with this annoying pain (the neuralgia), which got to where it felt like a light bruise-burn. It didn't exactly feel like a bruise. It didn't exactly feel like a burn. It felt like both. But, again, there were areas where there would be acute pain—wherever the weight of my skin pressed down on or pulled on damaged nerves (whether I was upright or laying down). For some time, those pains were so stressful. I stopped taking the Gabapentin® early on because it wasn't helping me all that much. Again, to my chagrin, I was not allowed to have any opioids or effective painkillers and I was at the doctor's office more than once. The painkillers are around. I just didn't get any. I asked him for pain relief, but did not note any specific drug and maybe I should have asked for something specific (but I didn't know the names of painkillers).

It's a good thing I didn't initially go to a hospital, which is not to say someone shouldn't do that. Had I gone to the hospital, I would have been there for a while. Some people with shingles go to a hospital and end out with a very hefty bill. All hospital bills are expensive, these days. Every little thing gets tallied. My Primary-Care physician handled the problem just fine. I didn't even think of going to a hospital, but with other people, they just assume that they must go and so they automatically go. A few by way of the emergency room. They generally don't get turned away, but they could be advised to go to Primary Care, right away, instead. Still, all patients have to start on the anti-viral medicine right away and they will get this at the hospital and by way of emergency care.

I did not go to a hospital but some people have. Again, the office people at the doctor's got me in fast, once I had seen the shingles. My seeing the shingles had actually taken me a while since I had genuinely thought I'd passed a gallstone and that this was why I had the pain. Again, only when I went to take a shower did I see the ugly pustules. The moral of this story is—always <u>well</u> investigate your pain whether it is slight, moderate, or more severe. When I told my doctor that I'd initially thought I'd had a gallstone that passed, he respectfully laughed (at least, he seemed to have been being respectful). He was, for sure, amused by my guess.

I'd had no clue what was besetting me because I'd never had anything like shingles and I'd never known anyone who had had shingles. I didn't really even know what shingles was—and here I was, an older person. In the back of my mind, I may have just thought they were a type of rash that wasn't too besetting or upsetting. I surely did find out otherwise. I had no clue how they were caused. I got caught unawares, as so many people do.

Some people who have had COVID (or a variant or sub-variant of COVID-19) claim to have had upper respiratory nasal problems so they were regularly blowing their nose. This could be a secondary infection or condition of COVID. There can be primary or secondary conditions and symptoms related to shingles, too (or any medical condition, for that matter). A secondary condition can occur because of the more major malady or disease. Symptoms will relate to the major malady or disease, and different symptoms will relate to the secondary condition. Often, a secondary condition will come upon someone because the major malady or disease has weakened the immune system. However, there are times when different people will have differing symptoms when they have the same major malady or disease, which is why all symptoms get listed when it comes to medical reporting. There could be ten symptoms on the list, for example, but people who have the major malady or disease may only end out with a few of those symptoms. Some symptoms may be more common, however, with some medical issues, like breathing problems are with COVID, or pustules are with shingles. It is important to try to distinguish between what is primary and what is secondary, when diagnosing or assessing diseases or ailments. To some extent, secondary conditions can relate to any treatment given, too. Something can flare up, because of the treatment for the primary condition. Sometimes symptoms can stay around, even after a virus seems to be beat. People have complained about Long COVID, meaning that certain symptoms of COVID are still with them, even though they are not testing positive for COVID. The symptoms are not usually all that bad, but they can be hard to cope with and can slow down and interrupt a person's life. The virus can be overpowering and have this after-effect, for a time and even indefinitely. Less acute upper-respiratory symptoms can stay around. Breathing can be less effortless. Malaise and fatigues can be experienced. Long COVID is something steady and will be there every day. Shingles causes fatigue. More sleep I needed when you have shingles. Probably, all viruses make you tired because they wear down the body. You get tired blood.

With shingles, I have often wondered if the presence of the virus can make people a little more tired, at times. Does its presence contribute, at all, to fatigue? When it is hot, I sense the shingles virus does not like it and might react in the body, some. I suspect the shingles virus can be responsible for starting up a rash or adding to an already-started rash. It can only be a suspicion. I sense that it could occasionally move around in the body and that it is not in all cells but the cells it is in tend to prefer certain areas. It has been medically documented that the virus likes the backbone area. I wonder if it might like the back area of the upper neck where the neck meets the head. I wonder if there could be groups of this virus living in two or three different areas. It would be great if come kind of shot could come into being that would kill that chickenpox virus (that becomes the shingles virus), once it settles in the body. It lives dormant for years. Some viruses in the body can be killed off, but not this virus.

Does some of the COVID virus stay in a body and is that why some people have Long COVID? Could any of the COVID immunizations or boosters be causing Long COVID or what appears to be Long COVID? They have a ways to go when it comes to virus research. Nobody likes anyone using animals to do this. Animals get way over-used in labs. Some get used for common-sense and obvious-answers experiments. Some get used in more than one place because results are not adequately consolidated, from place to place, area to area and country to country. Perhaps all this research here, there, and everyone should be internationally consolidated and a large international center should be built (since we all have the computer now). If all was put into one central data place, more animals would be spared pain and suffering. All would be consolidated and given 'other language' interpretation so experiment results could be seen and therefore not repeated or duplicated. Much could be done, much faster.

As noted before, pustules, with shingles, cannot be considered to be a rash. Having nerve problems under the skin is not associated with rashes. A rash is tiny or small bumps on the skin. Pustules are huge blisters. A rash heals up fast, with proper treatment care. Pustules hang around much longer. They are ugly, too, and extremely sensitive to the touch. Do not be idealistic and think that shingles pustules will go away fast, like a general rash can.

In time, will better immunizations/vaccinations come to the front for COVID? They could. There could be more types of treatment that pass necessary inspections, too. Shingles has good immunization types, already, but like with anything, this can improve. The immunizations for COVID was government-sponsored to begin with and different governments footed the bill. Needless to note, it all added up, big time. The different country governments step in, when there are pandemics. The day comes when they step out and when citizens have to foot the bill for their own immunizations bills, like they have to foot bills for medical care and hospital care when a person comes down with the malady or the disease. COVID cost citizens considerable money, relative to clinic and hospital bills. The insurance companies ate some of those costs. (They had many life insurance pay-outs, too.) Fortunately, many older people had MediCare and other people had insurance coverage for medical, too. Some did not, though. Immunizations have cost the different world governments considerable money.

However long a country has a pandemic will determine how long a government is obligated to foot the immunization bill, to care for its people. Any selected immunization(s) go through testing and clearances. Some had been rushed and some were not so rushed. Anything related to the chickenpox and shingles shots came about more slowly (and were stamped 'safe' for public use), unlike the immunizations for COVID, which came about faster. 'Healing' shots for COVID were slow to come around, essentially because of politics. Nothing much was on the News about any of these remedies or possible remedies. Nothing much was ever noted about research, either. There was much on about the immunizations, but little on about the cure when people had COVID. Hospitals had difficulty coping. Many people died really fast and sometimes, there weren't enough hospital beds. There was often a shortage of medical staff. Many hospital workers ended out with COVID because they were continually exposed to it. All these workers became heroes to other people. Some of them went the extra mile, many times.

Over time, the COVID immunizations might improve. More medicines that present COVID deaths might come into play, too. All that is needed is one. Is there something better than using a form of COVID to fight COVID? You wonder if medicine remedy for certain other viruses will help to work against COVID. Does America have enough lab workers and researchers to work against and contend with all the viruses that are in and around America? On the subject of shingles, preventing early chickenpox is very important to do, world-wide. Perhaps more medical research about shingles will yield better immunizations and medical treatment. Parents should talk with school health officials about prevention, and somehow and some way seek out the immunization for their children. Would a shingles immunization react badly with a COVID one? It is not good to get certain immunizations at or near the same time as getting other immunizations. Many immunization types have to be staggered. Always check any and all timings out with a doctor. Some shots do not have to be staggered (with ample time between them) and doctors will know what to advise).

PART 4
Pain, slow healing, and final healing

To emphasize, during the latter stage of shingles, it can be frustrating because the neuralgia takes so long to go away. In the meantime, there are times when an area can be really painful, and you moan. You can re-shift your position and that can bring some relief to an area but note I use the word, some, because it is not complete relief, at least not immediately. After several months went by and I could finally lay on my back, when I laid down, the area where the blisters had been felt tight, relative to the area that was facing towards the ceiling when I was on my back. So many days can go by and there is just no change at all in your condition. A rash goes away fast. A bruise goes away fast. Most cuts do, too, but nerve damage associated with shingles heals ever so slowly.

You keep expecting the affected areas to all heal up fast, but they don't. The pain and irritation stays around way too long. It's different, and frustration about it can be constant, and last a long time. Weeks go by, and you can notice no change at all and that is not an exaggeration. In fact, I'm not exaggerating anything, relative to my recording of my shingles experiences. Shingles are truly awful. It was a horrible experience. It would have gone easier for me if I'd only got them in one spot, and maybe somewhere else besides my upper torso (front and back areas) because my sleep was always affected.

It is patience-stretching to have the neuralgia around way longer than you expected it to be. Neuralgia will, of course, vary from case to case. Mine just really dragged on. Again, I believe the discomfort and pain kept raising my temperature a little and making me more tired. It, really, was exasperating. My cells had to have been going through considerable disturbance all along the way, even towards the end (six months later, or more). This could be why some people end out getting cancer after they've had shingles—i.e. it is this cellular

71

disarray. This is why you must eat well, and rest. Eventually but after some time, the subsiding goes past a certain point and you are, pretty much, home free.

I was happy when I could <u>finally</u> lie down on my back. I could sleep on my back sooner than I could on my front (which I never, really, do anyway). The front area was all over that right rib area. I prefer sleeping on my back all the time so my backbone will stay a little straighter. It took some time before I could lie on my back with no pain, though. At first there was discomfort, but eventually there was only mild discomfort and I did not notice it, so much. Any shifting and turning was still problematic, though. When that time of minor versus major discomfort when lying down on my back finally came, it made a huge difference. What a relief. My life started to get better. It felt like I was recovering. Even when this welcomed time finally came, though, I was still needing to rest more than usual. It seems like fatigue is a predominant symptom of shingles, and that it is present all along the way and even to the very end of the ordeal. As the neuralgia subsides, the fatigue subsides.

With the shingles, I was <u>always</u> more tired than usual, even at around twelve months. At six months, it was more like I had to rest more than sleep, but I needed more sleep than usual, too. Any extra heat didn't help the situation, either. Added heat slows you down, anyway. My shingles were predominantly late spring and early summer ones (around a desert area). I couldn't wait for the fall, but when fall came, I still felt some discomfort and pain over the top part of my rib area (but not quite as much in the back area). Even when winter came around, this was still somewhat the case.

I also noticed that, to some extent, I lost a little more of my hair than usual during my shingles ordeal. Fortunately, it wasn't too much, but it was some and I'm not sure why that was. I certainly did notice it. It was the hotter months, and, the shingles were stressful and either of those situations could have had something to do with the extra amount of hair loss. Either or both (heat/stress) could cause a little hair loss, and lack of certain vitamins could have, as well. Laying down more than usual because of continual fatigue, and sleeping more, could be the cause of a little extra hair loss, too, because your head rubs against

72

the pillow more. I noticed a little more of my hair coming out for several months. One or both prescriptions could have affected my hair follicles, too. I just don't know whether that was the case, or wasn't. The hair loss is a bit of a mystery. Could it have been happening because of the shingles? It was not on any symptoms list I was given. (**You must always read the symptoms list for any medicine/medication you take.** I even underline some of the content on those pages.)

Hair loss is known as alopecia. Men deal with hair loss more than women do, as a whole. There is male-pattern baldness many men have to contend with and some will have hair transplanting done, which certainly helps. Hair from a lower area is transplanted to the top area. Losing hair, for both men and women, tends to occur more around the top area of the head.

When women get older, they can lose some hair, and have alopecia, which can be bad, and can be hard on the ego. Eating a balanced diet is key. You don't want to go without certain vitamins for too long a period of time. When there is extra hair loss, the person well knows it. When the afflicted person combs their hair, there will be more strands than usual and this will be constant and will lead to a helpless panic.

Alopecia is a type of affliction and the person will need to see a doctor about the condition. Changing shampoo and conditioner may be necessary. Eating enough dairy, citrus fruit, and green leafy vegetables (like spinach) is, for sure, important to do. Taking certain vitamins can help. In my case, it almost seemed like some of the shingles virus went up to my head and scalp area. It really did seem that way. The virus in my body had to go somewhere. I know it usually goes to the backbone. Supposedly it went over to my backbone but I couldn't help but wonder if this un-welcomed virus went up to my scalp area. The lower part of my head area, in back, tended to itch quite a lot and I got small bumps down in that back area. This had never happened before. At times, the top part of my head seemed a little more irritated, too, but that was barely noticeable. So, what was I to think? I couldn't think anything specific because I had no answers. This could have been heat-related, though.

Perhaps the hair loss I experienced was just a coincidence. Perhaps all of the virus really did return to my backbone, to quietly reside (but it did seem like some of it was in the lower back area of my head because that area, which never itched before, started to itch). The hair loss mainly occurred after the pustules had completely gone (but it occurred soon afterwards). That could have been when I first noticed it, though. It could have started earlier than that. I know the virus is still living in my body. Perhaps more research will be done on where any and all of the shingles virus can travel to and settle in the body. Does it always go live around the backbone, in other words? Or has it been known to go to other places? The virus needs a nerve trunk to survive. Does the virus split up and go to more than one area? There really is not that much concrete information out about shingles. There's general information but it is not in-depth.

There was no scarring from the shingles pustules, either. It is when there is a lot of scratching on the skin that there is a risk of scarring. Certain vitamins can reduce or somewhat prevent scarring. Biotin especially helps with that. Anyone who has shingles should be taking a good multi-vitamin, every day. Calcium is one vitamin that is needed, too. It would be good to see a nutritionist early on, if you ever have to go through shingles. Some people can't afford a nutritionist so they have to go to books or the Internet.

To emphasize, if you live with or around another person, it's possible that if you have shingles that someone else you are in contact with can get chickenpox but only if any of the pustules break open. The liquid inside them is what can be contagious; it holds the live virus and touching that liquid can cause someone to come down with chickenpox. This can be very bad for pregnant women. Until the blisters have crusted over and are completely dried up, they could cause viral transference when any liquid is touched.

Because the liquid in the blisters can end out causing actual chickenpox in people who are exposed to that liquid, shingles is considered to be an infectious disease, as is the chickenpox. The odds are not super-high that someone will touch the liquid, but it can and does happen. Married or paired-up couples have to be careful about this happening. Just accidentally touching the closed blisters might be okay (but never take that chance). If any of the blisters have leaked liquid <u>anywhere</u> on the body, the liquid can be contagious. Any clothes can get the liquid on them, too; the liquid can go through clothing. The liquid could conceivably get on towels, too, after a bath or shower.

As noted earlier, the blisters or pustules do not seem to break open. They could, though. They are rather thick and in my case, they just seemed to dry up and the liquid seemed to get absorbed back into my body. I cannot swear to that happening, though, because in my case, they could have all broken open when I showered and the liquid would have been rinsed off by the rushing water and I wouldn't have even known it. If a pustule bursts open and there is liquid anywhere, once the liquid dries the virus that was in where the pustule was will die, but of course, the virus is still in your body. Once the liquid, itself, dries, the virus will always die. Viruses live in liquid and moist areas. They thrive inside bodies. They live in what is living. They do not live in a dry area very long, though some viruses can live in dry areas longer than other viruses can.

Maybe some research should be done and come out about medically-lanced blisters, and about whether or not lancing would be helpful and could conceivably remove at least some of the virus that goes back into the body and then moves about in the bloodstream. (Blood gets 'streamed' around the body because the heart pumps blood and blood is, therefore, moving around. Because the body moves around, blood moves around, too. All the blood doesn't exactly circulate, as in a circle, but it does have a movement pattern. Oxygen goes in with help from the coronary artery, it gets into the heart area and the bloodstream. Also, would medically lancing them, early on, cause there to be less nerve damage, and perhaps even cause any nerve damage to last less long? Another question is, does the virus stay about the same size, in the body? It doesn't seem to grow or increase, but maybe it can and maybe it does? Does the virus increase in amount, in the body? Maybe that is why people end out getting a flare-up of shingles? The virus increases or expands. What research have they been doing, relative to all these issues, I wonder. Mainly, why don't some people get a second bout of shingles after they've had the first bout and if they do, why is the second bout apt to be quite mild? (This is the usual pattern.) Does the anti-viral medicine that had been taken disable or cripple the virus that is in the body so it can no longer flare-up in full measure but only in a minor and hardly-noticeable way? Now there's a question. Some of these questions may already have answers; others may not.

What I know is that many Baby Boomers have been getting shingles, as are any of the younger groups if they, also, never had the chickenpox vaccine and it doesn't seem like there has been enough research done about shingles in preparation for this large number of people coming down the pike. To what extent are children being vaccinated against chickenpox at schools these days? (Which schools even sponsor the vaccine?) What vaccines are given, where? Parents, and the children, often get them all muddled up. There must be a shot record that is kept up to date and what the shots are protecting against should be written into the shot record. School nurses used to give shot records. It was a pocket-sized yellow booklet and nurses wrote in what shots were given and when they were given. Nurses are the ones who usually give the shots, unless there is a visiting doctor. Now that so many have been getting shingles, will there be more research? Some government funds regularly go out to people doing such research (and anything similar).

With shingles, again, the nerve pain is pretty bad. It is distracting and nerve-wracking. Yes, nerve damage is nerve-wracking and that is a pun. It wracks your nerves. Again, any nerve pain will vary in intensity, depending on what position you have been in and because of gravity push and pull and pressure on the areas where there is nerve damage.

Any pain goes from strong pain, irritating pain, discomfort pain, general discomfort, and then mild discomfort, when you have shingles. Discomfort pain is annoying, distracting, and noticeable. Everyone has discomfort pain from time to time. It's not strong or acute pain, but it is pain. After three months, the discomfort pain especially cropped up after I'd been lying down on my good side, which I still had to do, even at three months. When I was on my good side, resting, at times I only had discomfort, not discomfort pain. You can still be aware of just discomfort, though. It can get to you. One thing about discomfort, is that you can usually live around it and survive OK. It's the pain that is the problem. You can be set back and overwhelmed because of pain. You may not be able to live with it, and function.

Discomfort pain would occur in a different spot when I was sitting down versus when I was lying down. It occurred wherever skin was pressed or pulled down in some way on any of the nerve-affected areas. It would stay around for a while and then subside and not be too noticeable as long as my position and incline didn't change so there would be no further pressing or pulling of the skin in and around the areas where the damaged nerves were. Any discomfort pain gradually got better as time went by.

I sensed, at three months, based on how slow the nerve damage had been healing, that it would be several more months before it would all completely go away (assuming all of it was going to go away and some of it wasn't going to be permanent). <u>Shingles heal so slowly because any affected damaged nerves heal slowly.</u> Shingles really tries your patience. <u>You become a more patient person after you have gone through the shingles experience.</u> You become a more patient patient (of the doctor's), and is that where the word, patient, comes from? A patient has to be patient, because of a, b, c reasons. There are other diseases that, also, bring about nerve damage but so much will depend on where the nerve damage occurs as to how it will affect the afflicted person. Nerve damage, especially when the afflicted area is larger, is very problematic. Sometimes, cortisone is given for nerve damage, but some people say "stay away from cortisone because it can really mess you up". You have to look before you leap when it concerns cortisone. Read a lot about it first. It has its benefits—just be careful.

Probably for men, by six months any shingles and nerve pain and discomfort will, most likely, be almost gone or gone. For women, if the shingles were on the front area, because of the weight and pressure from the breast on the side the shingles are on, the nerve pain and discomfort in that front area may last considerably longer. Again, though, shingles can show up on a number of different places on the body. Some shingles cases are less problematic, and much milder. Some people are free of nerve damage pain sooner. There's just so many variables and every case is different. More cases tend to be less problematic. The large somewhat circular front and back type of case could possibly be the worst. Again, usually there are two body spots or areas being affected, and both are on one side of the body (on the front and/or back areas).

For me, as noted before, the last spot to heal was the line area right under the right breast. It's where the most pain and aggravation ended out being, in the end. (Even a year later, there was still some pain there and after a year and two months, everything was generally back to normal.) At around one year, there was slight tenderness in spots. I don't know if it was my imagination but the areas always felt warmer than other body areas did. When nerves get inflamed, are they, then, warmer? This was something I wondered. Something else I wondered about was 'exactly what on Earth is that wicked virus doing to those nerves to cause such pain and/or irritation'? How are they affecting the under-the-skin nerves, in other words? There are times when you sure wish you were a particular kind of doctor.

Even close in to a year, damaged nerves were constantly being compromise right under my left breast. When two body areas are next to each other and one area covers some or part of the other area, it is medically known as intertrigo. With front-area shingles, the weight of the breast presses down on the upper rib area where nerve damage is and this pressure causes constant irritation and pain (and lack of healing). There is intertrigo there. For me, it was hard to even go anywhere because of that problem. Again, there were times when I only wore a whole slip and not a bra. Wearing only a slightly snug slip (with upper stitching that contoured the upper area) helped bring about some relief but not total relief. The pain there was constantly frustrating, and there was nothing I could do about it. The area kept getting aggravated, over and over and over and this was hard on my state of mind. It is such a slow recovery with shingles, anyway.

Anyone who gets shingles, at whatever age, is in for a lengthy and very unpleasant experience. Special medical treatment and help will be needed, and needed right away. Keep in mind that a few younger people, and children, can get shingles, so parents, realize that shingles can show up as one or more patches of large blisters or pustules. A doctor has to determine if an individual has chickenpox, or shingles. When blisters are seen, remember to not touch them, or pop or lance them. Again, when a pustule dries, whatever had been inside that had been liquid, will die. The pustules are not merely a rash. There's a lot of liquid in them.

Parents who see any pustules or blisters on their children will be very upset and may not know what to do. Instinct tells them that something is bad enough that they have to get their child some quick medical treatment. Some children may have been sick to begin with. They could, for example, have been suffering from leukemia. A child with leukemia is very vulnerable to getting shingles if they've had chickenpox. Japanese scientists were able to develop a vaccine that inoculated children from getting shingles when they were leukemic. It prevents severe cases and was discovered at least forty years ago. It is not quite the same as the chickenpox immunization. The USA medical world has to pay close attention to what goes on, medically, in other countries. Everything can potentially affect the USA. Parents have to pay very close attention to inoculations for their children and keep up on any new information about them. Children usually aren't responsible enough to do this, so parents have to.

Even if a patch of shingles is small, it will be painful. If anyone of any age gets shingles around their face and eyes, they will have to go see a specialist, and perhaps two specialists. Shingles may not be easy to diagnose, around an eye area. Most people don't even know what the shingles are when the virus attacks the eye area. Do not wait for the eye problem to go away on its own. Get medical care immediately. Prescriptions will very definitely be needed.

For a week or two, if a patient's doctor will prescribe a painkiller, great; if not, go with the Tylenol® 500. With time, always go to a lower strength with any prescription and with any over-the-counter drug or medicine/medication. Don't ever take more of a prescription than is needed and keep close tabs on the dosage and how much you are taking. Dosage amount, in the U.S., is usually determined by number of milligrams of the drug or main acting agent.

Also, only finish up a prescription if the doctor insists you do because there are some prescriptions you can get that could be more pills or capsules than you need for the ailment. You, only, ever, want what medicine or medication you need. You never want excess, only what you really need, but if you need to take all that is in the bottle, and even need a second prescription, so be it. Take the pills. Be in charge of what you <u>know</u> you need, not what you think you need and not what you think you want. Be very discerning, when it comes to prescription drugs. Protect your body. Stay accurate. Do what the doctor says.

Shingles will set any person back. Anyone afflicted will feel like they're going through the wringer, and later, like they've been through the wringer. They won't be quite the same afterwards. All along the way, as previously noted, someone who has shingles will have to take care of themselves, if they are an adult. Early on, it is good if someone is around to help them. Still, there's only so much a helper can do. It is not easy to have to live with shingles. I think that I have made that point quite clear. Again, though, so much depends on where the virus decides to go and attach itself on the body.

In hindsight, because the nerve pain and discomfort took so long to go away, I suppose it was just as well I had no opioids. At the time, I wanted them, and I actually did need them at some point during the ordeal. I would have been glad to have had something on the mild side. I was forced to weather the storm, without taking any decent opioid painkiller. It was hard, though. Anyway, hats off to my doctor. (Be true to your school.)

I really have to wonder if living in a warmer climate might have ended out causing the nerve damage to be around for a longer period of time. When I got the shingles, there was a long stretch of higher heat than usual during April,

May, June, and July. I live in a desert climate and these are Global Warming times. Body temperature is higher when it is warm outside. It would make for an interesting study, relative to nerve-damage healing, to factor in external temperature as the nerve damage is going through a healing process since nerve damage is also common to other diseases and ailments. It would make for an interesting study, relative to the growth of viruses, too. True, the body tends to stay at a certain temperature, but it can have fluctuation variance, depending on what the external temperature is. What does this fluctuation variance mean, relative to the internal healing of shingles neuralgia?

Again and to emphasize, there are immunizations that will help you and keep shingles at bay. When you reach a certain age (if you aren't there already), look into having the one or the other immunization. Write it down as a 'to do' somewhere so you don't forget. Put it on your calendar. It is very possible that if your immune system is weak, for whatever the reason, that your having a live-virus vaccine could be problematic, but check with a physician about that before you have a shingles shot and regardless of how old you are. There is a live-virus shingles shot and one that is dead-virus so, again, check both out.

As a reminder, if you have children, get them in now to have the chickenpox vaccination. If your relatives, friends, or neighbors have children, advise those people to get the children in, now, to have the chickenpox immunization. Shout this from the rooftops. In my case, I didn't know anything about shingles or about any shingles vaccination. I got caught, unaware. I simply had never heard much of anything about shingles, which is why I did this short write-up—so more people would be aware of the overall subject, and the vaccinations.

Again, my ordeal finally came to an end about one year and a couple more months later but I wish I'd never had to go through it. What a setback. The real bad part was over with after about a half a year, but it was a little over a year before the residual part of it was generally gone (i.e. almost all of the nerve-damage healing had taken place). For a couple of more months, I still felt very slight sensitivity, though the feeling continued to diminish and then, it finally decreased to almost zero. The two areas still itched a little, though, which could mean that some nerves may not have been completely healed. After several years, there was just slight tenderness in the two areas so I have to assume that very slight and hardly-noticed damage will be a constant, in my case. I'm not sure, but it is possible I might not have as much feeling on my skin in the areas where the pustules had been.

I do not know if other people's shingles and accompanying nerve damage generally but essentially disappears after a full year, and a couple of months. I was all right after one year but that extra two months, for me, made a difference. Nothing around the two shingles sites was noticeably distracting, though there was still slight sensitivity. For some time, the area that had the pustules stayed pinkish (but eventually turned brownish), but I had no residual scarring from the shingles. Perhaps other people experienced something different but I'm generally healthy and I don't see how the residual nerve damage feeling couldn't go away, relative to other people, by around a one-year period of time. After a certain point, the nerve damage gets better and better but the way the virus attacks any nerve area makes it so the healing is gradual and really slow, even for the healthiest of bodies. The healing goes about as slow as a snail's pace.

For a time, I thought I would have some minor irreversible and noticeable nerve damage, which I would have for the rest of my life. (Even after one year, I still had some discomfort and the areas that had been affected felt tender.) In that there is only minor nerve damage now, it is barely felt. I have to assume the virus predominantly went back to the spine area and I am still feeling some pressure along one side of the backbone not far from where my back shingles pustules had been. Is the virus really living along my backbone—all of it? Or could some or all of it be living somewhere else? Also, why would it like living along a backbone? Does it feed on something there? Why does it like being around nerve trunks? You see, I have so many unanswered questions about shingles and I'm not sure there are any answers for most of my questions. We always know 'that' such and such is so, but we may not know 'why' such and such is so and again, it appears that more research needs to be done.

Again, I am left wondering if some of the virus may have gone up to the back of my neck and lower scalp area because those areas itch more and those areas are prone to getting a bit of a rash now, whereas they never had, before. The rash seems to occur because of the heat (combined with perspiration, perhaps). I am also wondering if heat and hot weather could be a contributing factor to activating the shingles virus and making it want to move around. Does heat contribute to the virus having stress so it thinks it has to relocate? If so, you'd think that hot showers would result in shingles, and I don't believe they do. I suspect that laying out in the sun might bother the virus. In any event, I got mine during the last week of March. As noted before, we got early heat that year. It was a hot summer. Global Warming has been doing that. Even when a room is cold, a bedroom, when sleeping, can get too hot because of the heater. You wonder, do more people from warmer climates get shingles, when compared with people in colder climates? Why is it there are few answers floating around, to questions about shingles? Has enough research been done, relative to shingles? Where is all the data? It seems like more could be done and put on record and given out to the public.

It's believed stress activates shingles. Heat can be a type of stress on and in the body's cells. The shingles virus likely does not like too much heat exposure (or maybe it does and that is why it feels free to move around)? If the virus becomes uncomfortable, does it perhaps go a little berserk and move around and re-situate somewhere else in the body and then voilà, there are the pustules?

The virus is dormant right now, supposedly along my backbone. Again, some of the virus could have gone up to my upper neck/lower head area, at the back where my hair is because that area itches and is prone to getting a rash more than it had been before. It could just be eczema or heat rash, though (since I live in a desert climate). Somehow, it just really seems connected to the shingles, though it may not be. I have always been prone to getting an occasional cold sore, but that is a different virus. It is similar, but a little different. I wonder if the two ever have anything to do with each other since they are both viruses and are both living in the same body. Could the activated shingles virus cause harm to the cold sore virus (one type of the herpes simplex) or have caused it to relocate so it no longer causes cold sores? Now, there is another question. Since I've had shingles, I haven't had any cold sores and that seems a little strange since I've gone through several winters now without even one cold sore and they tend to show up when my body gets real hot or real cold. (I used to get at least one or two per year, and now I get none per year.) It's distressing knowing viruses can live in your body, year after year. You never invited them in, and you can't evict them. They are as squatters. Viruses affect one another. One virus can beat another virus down and even cause it to disappear. To what extent the shingles virus is affected by the COVID virus and vice versa was not announced by medical experts, early on. Nobody on the News mentioned that but related research about that should be ongoing.

I have noted that after a year and two months that there is no residual nerve agitation but I still felt 'something' under my skin though any feeling is so minor that it is inconsequential. I suspect I'll always feel this but it is not distracting (unless I focus in on it, which I don't because it is just too minor now). So, again, I think there's been <u>very</u> slight nerve damage (sensitivity of the skin area), which is miniscule and hardly worth noting. I have to assume that the minor sensitivity is going to be permanent. It's so minor that it's not going to matter if it is. Have medical professionals ever done much research on continued neuralgia effects? What are the findings? No one ever hears anything about such subjects, but people want to know. Years later, it somewhat felt like there was less feeling on those once-affected areas. Those areas just feel 'different'. Could this mean that some of the nerves were slightly damaged?

What was strange about the remaining nerve-damage areas after about a year was that during the latter stage, the areas often itched and I'd have to scratch them. The itch was under the skin but it would first feel like it was on the skin. The two are totally different situations. Strangely, pressing down on the area gave it relief (never rubbing the area, though). Then I would move my hand away and it would, sometimes, start to itch again not long afterwards.

This got to be quite vexing. After twelve months, I still had a couple of spots that would sometimes itch, mainly when any weight of my skin would press or pull down on that area. I do not know why the areas would itch but I suspect it has to relate to the nerves. The nerves weren't completely healed but they were healed, generally. Like with so many other related issues, I suppose the itching issue is a mystery for medical experts to solve. People in different fields of Medicine will have a field day figuring out some of these mysteries. Areas that would more specifically deal with these kinds of issues would be Neurology, Micro-biology, Virology, Immunology, and Pathology. Pathology relates to studying and inspecting blood and blood samples.

There is still research to be done in the area of Neurology, Micro-biology, Virology, Immunology, and Pathology with regard to diseases that are associated with nerve damage, but nerve damage can still be present when there has been no disease. The fewer animals that are used in nerve-related research, the better, as far as many people are concerned. There is too much repetition and duplication and non-sharing of results when using any-sized animals for any animal research. Too much research gets done, using animals, when the results are easily predictable and have common-sense results and those tests never had to be and it is awful when they are done. There is too much false rationalizing about many of these animal tests and results, too. Outside people see through all the weak rationale. Hopefully, tests can be done in the areas of shingles and neuralgia without using animals.

There hasn't been much national awareness out there about shingles and neuralgia. Few people even know about the shingles shots. Schools haven't been all that diligent about educating children and young people about shingles and neuralgia, either. How much they teach about chickenpox probably depends on the school. The chickenpox vaccine was given in the schools for a while but it may not be given in all schools today. It depends on the state, and the school district. Parents and guardians have to check this out.

Immunizations are not only given in schools, but they are also given at health-care centers and at doctor's offices, by a doctor or nurse (usually a nurse).

Not all schools around the nation give the same shots. It is up to the State, and also the locality, as to what shots at the different schools are mandatory. Some immunizations are boosters because some boosters (to the first or second shot in a series) are required or needed. Actually, immunizations begin in infancy. From birth to two years, many different immunizations are given. Very young children even get shots, right after birth. Shots are given before and during school attendance because so much contagion goes on at schools.

It gets confusing—some shots are given free (or used to be) and some are not. Some immunizing is done at schools or for school populations at a designated site. If they are not legally mandatory, doctors will solicit schools business so more children will know about and come in for shots. Parents will be alerted, in many cases, about shot availability. Some parents are phobic about shots, or they are misinformed (including about the COVID immunization series). Some parents do not want their child or children to have any shots, or to have certain shots.

Some parents think they can wait, but no, they can't. Babies, children, and teenagers have to be protected against measles, diphtheria, pertussis or whooping cough, chickenpox, mumps, et al. (now including COVID). It falls on parents to oversee that their children get all required and necessary immunizations <u>on time</u>, even if they have to pay for some of them. It is up to the whole community, though, to make sure the children in their area are up on all their shots, and that they are, too. It is also up to daycares, schools, providers (as doctors, nurses, and other health professionals), and even churches to unite in a campaign to get everyone fully vaccinated. Still, the immunization ball is always in the court of the parents.

If perchance a child, young person, or even adult is behind in getting needed immunizations, they can still get caught up and get any that they need. Some could be free. (They all should be free, many believe, or, at least, certain ones should be.) Certain diseases, if not intercepted, can lead to permanent debilitating problems, like deafness, bad vision, poor reproduction, organ damage, blood problems, poor brain functioning, and respiratory problems.

Some lead to a quick death, or a premature death. Health has to be maintained via these shots, like a car has to be maintained. Human life is at stake.

All immunizations have to be staggered. There is a sequence to them. Some are done in a series, and dates given tend to be four to six weeks apart (but ask a professional about that, relative to any and all shots). Otherwise, different shot types are given at different ages. Teenagers have to have specific immunizations, especially one against tetanus. Getting all helpful immunizations for minor children involves choice on the part of parents, but it involves motivation, too. The COVID immunization is available for tweens or pre-teens and teenagers. It was made available to babies in the summer of 2022. The government footed the COVID bill. Again, immunizations have to be staggered. Some cannot be given on top of other immunizations. Certain ones can be given at the same time, but certain ones can't. Blood in bodies has to have time to assimilate vaccine content, which has to gradually settle in.

Certain shots should be mandated everywhere because if people aren't vaccinated against a, b, c, etc., they can come down with one or more diseases and become contagious and cause disease spread that goes far and wide. A disease can even be put upon someone who is vaccinated. They could carry the bacteria or virus, for a time, and be contagious, though they might only have a mild form of what they had been exposed to. Certain immunizations used to be more mandated for children. Now, it is all very random—too random—relative to what is mandatory in the different states and localities.

Immunizations are a biological product; they cost money. Even so, again, anyone can catch up on missed immunizations and they should, which includes the chickenpox vaccination (and having the shingles shot, if necessary).

Young people of all ages should learn about immunizations and diseases when they are young. They should take it upon themselves to do that, and only partly depend on others. Young people really have to be on their toes these days, about this, that, and the other. So much is going on . . . .

As an aside, I actually feel sorry for young people. They have many diverse (non-physical) handicaps and there are more limitations put upon them. The world can be too hard to understand for too many years. They learn too many wrong things and not enough right things about this and that. They tend to be less humble and less appreciative than the young people of yesteryear were— not all are, but on the whole, they are. They are a product of their environment, but some young people choose to be as islands and they think for themselves. They break away from crowd and mob thinking, which has hold of many. Some are able to become their own person, which is usually more medically and psychologically healthy, when kept in balance. Balance in life is more calming. I missed being taught certain things that were important when I was young. (Possibly, I expected my mother to relay too much.) My father was always working. Still, I learned a lot from both of them. <u>I wish I would have learned enough earlier on, though, so I would have been able to dodge more bullets than I did, throughout my life.</u> One of those bullets was shingles. I was caught by surprise. If I'd just had that shingles prevention shot, I would have been spared considerable pain and suffering and actually, loss of valuable time concerning my writing, and work.

Perhaps my parents didn't know much about shingles, but you'd think they would have. I do not recall either parent ever having had shingles. I would have known it if they'd had it, too. Everyone in my immediate family knows such things about the other family members. I would have known if either had come down with shingles, even when I wasn't living with them because we all kept up with one another, especially about something like that. I'm quite sure that no one in my family ever got shingles. Just me.

I am out some valuable time, indeed, because I had to rest and sleep so much more than I usually did. I can never get all those hours back. They were valuable, because I write so much. I still have some miles to travel, with my writings. I try to eat better now, but I would have done that, anyway. The only silver lining that I can see is that I was able to write this short book, which I hope will be of some help to others. Too few know much about shingles, sadly, and this book will help to inform people because it is this book that records what I actually experienced and some of my thoughts about shingles.

I'm more concerned about possibly getting cancer now, too, because my immune system had been so compromised. Since the shingles ordeal, I haven't quite felt as well as I did before so I'm going to have to pay even closer attention to my health. Without good health, your day-to-day life can deteriorate. People can lose their good health at any time. In the more prosperous countries, there are more doctors per person, and more hospitals and medicines/medications per person. I was fortunate I had a Primary-Care doctor to go to, and that he took care of my medical needs. The U.S. has a high doctor-to-patient ratio.

In poorer countries, people (usually those older) may have to go through the shingles ordeal without getting any medical treatment. Some of the poorer countries have immunizations, for children and adults. The United Nations World Health Organization oversees much of that. So does the Red Cross and other organizations, some of which are private companies. In the United States, there is a Department of Health in Washington, D.C. that oversees these matters. The Department of Education somewhat does, too. There is also a Department of Veteran's Affairs and a part of that organization covers health and medical-related issues. Also, there is the Center for Disease Control in the U.S. that stays on top of both viral and bacterial diseases, or they at least try to do that because some diseases can hit fast and hard and be difficult to manage. The effect one virus has on another virus can be very important in the field of Virology. They are starting to look into multiple interactive virus behaviors more and more because this relates to Immunology (and to the other related Medical fields).

Even when there are numerous health organizations around the world, it does not help to have wars going on around the world. They breed disease because of what they are and what they do. Russia forced war on Ukraine in 2022, for example, and this caused many to leave, though many stayed. When buildings get bombed (and Russia blitzed Ukraine), utilities stop working so water, gas, electricity (heat and refrigerated food), and much else is not available. People starve and die. Garbage and sewage gets out of whack so people get sick from disease. Wars are not good for immune systems. When there are wars, many die from generally being ill, from starvation, and because they get too cold or too hot. Roads and bridges get destroyed so supplies cannot get in Stress (from fear and all the deprivations) can cause illness, too. It would certainly bring about shingles cases because shingles tends to be activated by stress. Many say that excess heat and/or cold stresses the shingles virus so that it reacts in the body. Apparently the shingles virus, because it is a living entity, does not like chaos or being uncomfortable. How it reacts to the prescribed medicine that people with shingles take would be interesting to observe under a microscope, especially when you realize that the medicine doesn't actually kill the virus. The virus continues to live in the body.

Again, it is mainly those who are 50 and older who tend to get shingles, but they especially seem to show up in seniors in their 60s and 70s. Chickenpox, itself, is a whole nother matter. People of all ages can get chickenpox, but children especially tend to come down with it. Chickenpox has to be diagnosed by a physician because other diseases or ailments can resemble chickenpox. On occasion, a blood test might be needed.

Viruses are very tricky. Each virus type or offshoot is different. The different viruses impact people differently and people can respond differently to them. Generally, older people do not respond so well to viruses. Their immune system has usually weakened, because they are older. They could have had any number of ailments over the years that could have weakened their immune system. The coronavirus or COVID-19 (and variants and sub-variants), specifically, is a good example of this. It, more often, takes the life of older people, although anyone at any age is vulnerable to getting the coronavirus (COVID) and dying from it. The shingles virus tends to flare up with older people, and so such flare-ups tend to relate to weakened or compromised immune systems. After and because of a shingles flare-up, and because of fighting the virus, do a person's blood cells build up new immunities against the shingles virus because their body fought off the shingles virus (i.e. the Varicella-zoster virus)? Could that be possible?

After a person is able to fight off the coronavirus, their immune system seems strengthened so it is more apt to fight off another exposure to the coronavirus (or is it that the virus, itself, is weakened and 'beat up' so it loses activity and cannot flare up?). This could perhaps be the case with the shingles virus, because if it ever returns, it only shows up in a milder form, whether someone gets a shingles shot after the have a main case of shingles, or don't. Does a major first flare-up end out killing some of the virus in the body, or end out weakening the virus so it cannot ever flare up, full-force, again? Why is it that after a strong initial flare-up, it seems to reduce the possibility of a second occurrence and renders a second occurrence less potent? Something had to have happened to the virus. Does its structure change? What gives?

You wonder, too, if the Varicella-zoster virus affects the coronavirus, or COVID, in any way, shape, or form (or if the reverse holds true). Do any viruses have an effect on COVID? If so, how would they affect it? How would these affects be recorded? How do all these viruses replicate or mutate, too? How do they dissipate, weaken, and get re-directed in the body? Does another virus in the body retard or stop any process, relative to another virus? What are invading viruses? Which ones are able to be killed inside of a body? And what other viruses are able to live in the body for years and not be of any immediate harm (like with the shingles virus)? Do two different viruses ever unite in the body and become more forceful? How do variants and sub-variants come about? They relate to a first virus but they can be stronger or weaker than the first virus and even cause different symptoms. Are there really variants and sub-variants, some people have wondered. Aside from COVID-19, what other viruses have variants and sub-variants?

The shingles virus is an invading virus but it does not seem as dangerous as a number of other viruses are. Fighting a virus with a virus falls under the field of Virology. It can be a dangerous field to work in. Usually an immunization has only a percentage of success with a virus. For example, any immunization against the coronavirus (COVID) might end out only having around a seventy-five percent success rate (and the immune system must fight the rest). Can they ever improve on percentage success rates? Probably. Will they be improving on the shingles immunizations? Hopefully, they will. Once they come up with an immunization, they should keep trying to improve on it (but they will sometimes rest on their laurels and spend time and money on other endeavors). Governments support and aid much of this medical research.

With the Varicella-zoster virus, it stays in your body even after you get through the ordeal and the assumption is (whether it gets reduced or crippled or doesn't) that it goes back to living along the backbone areas (but again, I suspect it could also go up to the back of the neck and lower area of the back of the head, though I could be wrong and so do not quote that). What I am wondering is, since the Varicella-zoster virus is in the body and continues to live in the liquid of the body, would it fight an entering and invading virus like the coronavirus or COVID so there would end out being less devastation caused to the person by the coronavirus, or would the shingles virus work in unison with COVID (or one of its variants or sub-variants) and end out being more activated because of the coronavirus (COVID) so that there could be even more complications and devastation put upon the person. It's the Varicella-zoster virus viral friends, frienemies, or enemies to the COVID virus or any of its off-shoots. There is so much to research.

I hope Varicella-zoster would fight against COVID and weaken the effects of COVID in a particular body that is harboring the Varicella-zoster virus (and it would be seeing the coronavirus as an invader to its space). You also have to wonder about other virus types that would be forced to be in a similar position. Does the Varicella-zoster virus fight other kinds of invading viruses? Would any of the virus ever be able to unify with an invading virus, in any way? How do variants and sub-variants form, and why do they? The answers to these kind of questions can only be answered by the medical professional people (especially by those people in research). How far into all this research each of the medical and science branches are, as relates to both the older and newer-detected viruses is not generally known to the public. Because of intellectual-knowledge theft and other reasons, such information is secreted. In the main, all countries keep their information about different viruses secret because of international espionage and theft and other reasons.

I can't help but wonder what Interferon can do to certain known viruses. Interferon is a group of anti-viral proteins having a low molecular weight and it is usually produced by the cells of animals in response to the virus (according to Merriam-Webster dictionary). Interferon is used to fight viruses. It's been around since the late 1970s. A lab in southern California first worked on it. It may relate to the use of a parasite or a chemical. (Obviously, it is all very technical.) It is cellular injecting into the blood. Not only are new immunizations discovered and manufactured, but dose intervals and ranging has to be determined. Many strain studies are always going on, all around the world. Are they shared enough?

After one year and two months, I had put the shingles ordeal behind me but again, I still had slightly tender and irritated areas of essentially no significance in both front and back (where the pustules had been). The hardly-noticeable feeling was a livable situation and was not distracting. When I was able to sleep all right on my back and on either side, I was such a happy camper. I never sleep on my front, for a couple of reasons. One, I want my back to be flat and straight when I sleep and two, I had been sleeping on my front when I had had that one horrid gallstone drop that got temporarily constricted somewhere in my tubing, and so, right or wrong, I got spooked. This hesitation about sleeping on my front may have been totally unrelated to the incident, however.

Relative to my shingles, what is now good is that I'm essentially back to normal. I'm a little more tired than usual, but not too much more. This relates to the fact that I have less lung capacity because my stomach presses in on my lungs because of a car accident I was in. I had the diaphragm surgery, but my stomach slipped back up, years later so I now have breathing problems. Research continues to go on, reference immunization. The research is expensive and it takes time. I'm aging, too, and aging has its problems, which seem to accumulate as the years keep on going by. "Aging ain't for sissies", my father used to say. That is a popular adage that is likely stated by different senior citizens, from time to time. After I wrote this, I heard it being stated in the movie, *Quartet,* which is a touching film centering on senior citizens (and on music, especially opera). These films about older people are great. There are quite a few of them out but I have yet to see one that includes the subject of shingles, and I wish there was.

The shingles episode really wore me down and affected me, psychologically. I went about doing everything a little more slowly for some time, but I functioned just fine and still got things done (though I rested and slept more). I had not been <u>overly</u> inconvenienced during the ordeal, but I had been inconvenienced. I had been able to cope on my own without in-home care, but early on, it was difficult (because of the pain from the nerve damage that was so slow to get better). It would have been wonderful to have had some help. You can get through shingles on your own but if you have a bad case of it, working a full-time job can be very difficult and even impossible, especially if it is a physical or even semi-physical kind of job. A sit-down job would be so much easier on a person coping with shingles.

Being tired, and the neuralgia, are both, at least, a little handicapping. Unlike some diseases, though, you can manage shingles but if it gets to be too much, call in for help or go get help. With me, I ate boxed meals cooked in the microwave and did not cook until I stopped being so fatigued. I did much less work (home projects, etc.), because I was on my feet less. I only did what I absolutely had to do . . . and perhaps just a little more. I'm somewhat of a go-getter type, and I always do everything I can and will push myself when I must and go the extra mile, as well. Some of the fatigue I experienced was from the medicine/medication I took; some was from the shingles. Realistically, though, you can only do what you can do, when you are sick.

You can do what you need to do to get through the day if you have shingles but you can't do much more than that. Just rest a lot, and be careful about any exertion. Watching TV or rented films takes your mind off the pain and discomfort. Comedies are good, but do not let yourself become too much of a couch potato. Even sick people have to get up and move around, off and on, so their blood will flow well and circulate better. In a not so strange way, blood has to be exercised. The heart's functioning helps the blood to exercise. The heart has to be exercised.

Now, besides TV and films, we have social media, which will also help keep someone's mind off the pain and discomfort. There is the personal computer and laptop to use for this and that, as well (besides the Social Media). There is also the smartphone now. Don't become a desk potato, either, unless you use it for your livelihood. You can read, too. There's on-line books, and regular books. What is key is being pre-occupied, but keeping to a balance in life is very important. Don't get stuck in ruts to the point where there is no balance. For example, some people play way to many video games, watch too many movies, or will even read too much (though reading is super good to do). Also, you aren't in quarantine when you have shingles (except for at first). You can go out to various places. You just don't want to overdo it. Always keep in mind that you're going to get tired more quickly if you go out anywhere, so know your limitations, in advance.

Again, every case of shingles is different because flare-ups and pustules are in different areas and cover different-size areas. One thing you must do, though, is get under the care of a physician because shingles is a viral disease. The physician will help you and guide you. You may need a second anti-viral prescription, depending on the situation. You'll want to see the physician for follow-up, too, and if there are any complications during the ordeal, talk with the physician handling your shingles case. Some physicians will let you call them (or will call you back if you call and leave word). Some may not receive calls. Much is different now, after the opioid crisis and after COVID rolled in. Your physician has to know about any problems right away. Your physician will want everything consolidated on a record put in one place. If you go to an emergency clinic, your Primary-Care physician needs to know so be sure to give him (or her) all of any related details or have the records transferred in to the doctor's office. The physician needs to know about the shingles.

There are still more male than female doctors in the U.S. and around the world. Medicine is still a male-dominated field. For how much longer it will be, only time will tell. As far as I'm concerned, the memory part of physician's brains has to work really well, but, memories must also be kindled to remember this and that so it is good that we have the computer and all the medical knowledge that is stored within it (and stored inside of books). We will always need doctors, though, because they are in charge of individual cases and have the more advanced medical knowledge, training, and experience. Since people first began living on Earth, doctors have been needed. Medicine has been needed. Medicine has been needed. Medicine evolved. I make note of the History of Medicine in my book, *The Surgery Experience*, which is about any surgery experience, really. It is similar to this book, but it is longer. The medical field has come such a long way. Many mistakes have been made over the course of time but they got corrected as medical progress continued.

Finally, please forgive any repetition that could be in this book. I tried to make sure that anything repetitious was worked in within a different or a better context. When you write something generally medical and when you are experiencing a medical ordeal at the same time, you sometimes forget what you noted earlier, especially if you are not well, are under medication, and have to rest and sleep more often than usual. I struggled with repetition, somewhat, with my surgery book, too. I had to go in and do some revising. I've gone through both book and they are 'generally' okay. The repetition isn't too bad and sometimes, it is helpful. (I also wrote a short book about cataract surgery but that is a whole nother subject.)

Both books were written as I was convalescing (and somewhat written, thereafter). Both books are thorough, relative to my experiences. Neither book is perfect and so, please forgive. I was working on several books at a time, too. It became a little difficult to juggle everything but I've done my best for the time I have been allowed. Last, I hope you will spread around as much of this content about shingles as you can. Think—prevention. The more people there are who tell others details about shingles, the fewer people there will be who will have to suffer when they get them. Be sure to tell as many people as you can about the shingles shot, too.

INDEX

Printed in the United States
by Baker & Taylor Publisher Services